CARE
LESS
LIVES

CARE
LESS
LIVES

THE STORY OF THE RIGHTS MOVEMENT
OF YOUNG PEOPLE IN CARE

Mike Stein

Care Less Lives

Published by Catch22
Churchill House
142-146 Old St
London EC1V 9BW

A National Voice
Central Hall
Oldham Street
Manchester
M1 1JQ

Catch22. We believe every young person deserves the chance to get
on in life - no matter what.
The National Care Advisory Service, is part of Catch 22, we are the
national advice, support and development service focussing on young
people's transition from local authority care.
www.catch-22.org.uk
www.leavingcare.org

A National Voice - A National Voice is the only charity in England run
by and for young people from Care. We work to improve the Care
system by listening to what young people have to say and giving them
a voice with local and national Government. We believe that children
growing up in Care deserve the same supportand opportunity that
you would hope for any child.
www.anationalvoice.org

A catalogue record for this book is available from the British Library
ISBN 978-0-9570428-0-3

Printed in Great Britain by Wood Richardson Ltd, York
Design by Michael Elgie

CONTENTS

Chapter 1

Why Care Less Lives?

*'In all actions concerning children, whether undertaken by public
or private social welfare institutions, courts of law, administrative
authorities or legislative bodies, the best interests of the child shall
be a primary consideration.'*

Article 3, United Nations Convention on the Rights of the Child

Why Care Less Lives? The simple answer is that this book is about the *lives* of
young people in children's homes and foster care whose care has been *less* than
it should have been. But, as the subtitle, the *Story of the Rights Movement of
Young People in Care*, suggests, it also tells the story of how these young people
came together to share their experiences, and bring about changes in the care they
received – to make their lives *less care less*.

In the light of abuse scandals in children's homes, the idea of 'care' as offering
needy children a loving home is at best tainted and at worst derided, by the
public, by professionals and, not least, by those young people who suffered years
of ill treatment at the hands of their 'carers'. Perhaps we should refer to these
young people as 'survivors' of care although, sadly, that has not been the fate
of all. The tragic irony of their situation is that many of these children
were rescued from abusive or neglectful parents to be provided with 'care' in
their '*best interests*'.

However, such public scrutiny of care is very recent. It is only from the 1990's
that the horrific revelations of such wide scale abuses made headline news. Before
then, there were many high profile child welfare cases, as there have been since,
reporting the appalling suffering of *individual children* 'known to social services',

often at the hands of their parents. But there has been far less public interest in, or care about care *generally*: if there had been, we may not continue to be haunted by the legacy of abuse. The prevailing view of politicians was that 'care' was a service provided by councils through 'dedicated' residential staff and 'salt of the earth' foster carers to those unfortunate children who could no longer live with their parents.

But how did young people see and experience their 'care'? This book explores this question through the story of their rights movement in England, from its small beginnings in 1973 when the first group of young people living in children's homes began in Leeds, to the creation of a national organisation of young people in care in 1979, and its ongoing struggles today. However, before embarking on the story, some clarification of 'rights movement', as used in the subtitle, may be helpful.

The concept of 'rights' is widely used but far less defined. In this book, following the principles laid down by the United Nations Convention on the Rights of the Child[1], it will refer, first, to young people's right to *participation* in the decisions that affect them and influence their day-to-day lives; second, to their right to *protection* from violence and maltreatment wherever they are living; and, third, to their right to the *provision* of 'resources', or services to help them to fulfil their individual potential. Clarification of these 'rights', sometimes referred to as the '3 P's', will be given, as the story unfolds, through examples derived from young people's experiences, and be re-visited in the concluding chapter. At this stage, it will suffice to say that participation, in its many guises, from consulting a young person in care about their individual needs, to involving young people collectively in decisions that may influence many such lives, is central to this story.

In the context of human struggles, the idea of a rights 'movement' for young people living in care seems at first sight a little pretentious, as well as perhaps veering on the romantic. After all, we think of 'movements' as reserved for the great historical struggles, such as civil liberties, peace, labour, women – though not all social movements are as progressive. Yet, although large in numbers, these and other great movements are usually made up of the combined actions and endeavours of smaller local groups sharing similar goals. It is the local associations, branches, youth and community groups that are the bread and butter of national organisations. And these great movements do not suddenly appear - '*or rise like the sun at an appointed time*' - they are present at their '*own making*'[2]. They often have very small beginnings and come about through the beliefs and activities of a few.

Also, in most of these movements there are, over time, internal conflicts, including, sometimes, the battle for its soul, as well as changing membership, and supporters who strictly speaking are non-members but fellow travellers: the women against pit closures supporting the miners on strike, and, more globally, the white liberals supporting the black anti-apartheid struggle. By all these criteria, as this account will show, we can speak of a 'rights movement' of young people in care.

How did 'Care Less Lives' come about? It is, in the main, my reflections as an 'adult member' of the rights movement: Leeds *Ad-Lib*, Who Cares?, the National Association of Young People in Care (NAYPIC), and the early years of A National Voice. In this sense it is a personal account of a journey which I was fortunate to share with many resilient young people, as well as other adult supporters. During this journey I attended many meetings and events, and spent hours discussing the topics with young people. I also received and read many minutes, reports and papers: these have contributed in no small way to this story – and I hope have now been rescued from history's dustbin. Also, during the last five years I have interviewed some, but not all, of the main participants, both young people and adults. I owe a lot to a lot of people and hope that my reflections have done them justice, although they are not responsible for my judgements.

This book begins by describing the very parochial origins of the movement, when in 1973, a group of young people living in children's homes in Leeds, known as *Ad-Libbers*, came together for the first time to talk about their day-to-day experiences and to campaign to improve their lives in care. Although there was nothing new in the 1970's about youth groups or groups of youths – indeed, it has often been the mission of the former to recruit, educate and, from time to time, attempt to reform the latter – but Leeds *Ad-Lib* was a very different kind of youth group. After all, these were some of the most vulnerable young people in society, young people who had been abused or neglected by their families, or who had many difficulties growing up, and who were taken into care for their own welfare. The *Ad-Lib* group gave these young people a voice for the first time, all be it at a very parochial level.

The book continues by telling the story of how the *Who Cares?* Project 'spread the word' from its beginning in 1975 until its sudden ending in 1978. It relates how *Who Cares?* came about and how its activities led to the views of young people living in children's homes reaching a far wider public and professional audience, as well as the formation of regional groups of young people living in care in different parts of England. It also recounts how the *Who Cares?*

project came to an abrupt end in 1978, leaving young people without funding for future meetings, without leadership from within, or an organisation to further their cause.

The book describes how these difficult circumstances led, in 1979, to the setting up of the National Association of Young People in Care (NAYPIC), the first national organisation of young people in care in England. It discusses the activities of NAYPIC between 1979 and 1994, including its campaigns and surveys, the setting up of *Black and In Care*, and *Sharing Care*, its highly influential Evidence to the House of Commons Committee on Children in Care, and how its activities contributed to major changes in law, policy and practice. It also tells the story of how NAYPIC's struggles over funding and internal conflicts led to its demise in 1994, resulting in a five year period without any national organisation representing young people in care.

Following this hiatus, the book discusses the background to the creation of a new organisation for young people in care, *A National Voice*, launched in 1999. It describes its contribution to the rights movement for young people in care. This includes its regional road shows and *Amplify* fun event, its response to *Me, Survive Out There?*, the Government's proposals to reform the law for young people leaving care, as well as its campaigns to improve foster care, education, and accommodation for young people leaving care. Not to mention, its '*Bin the Bag*' fashion shows!

In conclusion, I will reflect upon a number of questions arising from this story. What impact did these young people's groups and organisations, collectively constituting their rights movement, have upon child welfare policy and practice during these years? What can we learn from a young person's history of care about their lives during this period? Why did their concerns about the abuse they experienced fall on deaf public, professional and political ears for so long? And, finally, what can we learn from their story – so the lives of young people today and tomorrow will be *less care less*?

Chapter 2

Ad-Lib
Voices from below

'Everyone was in complete agreement that the present system of children from children's homes being singled out by having their dinner money paid directly from the Corporation was degrading and embarrassing. It was unanimously agreed that you be asked by this group to change the policy and allow children to take their own dinner money weekly like other children do.'

(Request from the *Ad-Lib* group to the Director of Social Services, 1973)

How the *Ad-Lib* group came about

In January 1973, a small group of young people living in children's homes in Leeds came together with two workers to talk about their lives. It was the first time that a group giving credence to the views of young people in care had met. Bringing young people together to share their experiences, to be listened to, and to have their opinions respected, represented a very different approach to the established practice of the day - therapeutic group work which was dedicated to 'diagnosing', 'interpreting' and 'treating' the problems of 'patients'. In the Leeds group, the voice of the young person was to be more than a means to an end[3].

The early 1970's was a time of change, optimism and new ideas in social work. There were challenges to the psychodynamic world view that had fuelled the development of the child care officer's social casework and their preoccupation with individual problems and solutions. Advocacy, welfare rights, group and community work were increasingly seen as relevant to the plight of 'clients' confronted with a range of social problems, including poverty, homelessness and inner-city deprivation.

No longer could the internal and external worlds of those 'on the receiving end' be comfortably separated in how they were understood or responded to[4].

From the late 1960's, increased recognition of these social problems had also given rise to new pressure groups, such as Shelter and the Child Poverty Action Group, campaigning for changes to social policy, as well as wider social movements, including women's and civil liberties groups campaigning for more radical transformations of traditional social relations. But what was common to both these approaches was the recognition of the 'rights' of different groups: of the poor to a home and a decent income to provide for their children, of women to equal rights to men, and of black people to equal rights to white people in society. Not that there was any recognition at that time of the rights of children in care, or more modestly, any legal requirement for their views to be considered by those responsible for them.

It was in this context that the Leeds initiative came about. The idea of a group for young people in care had come from two child care workers, initially in response to questions by individual young people about leaving care, as captured in the page below from chapter one of the '*Ad-Lib In Care Group Story*'.

What is it like leaving care?
Do you have to go into lodgings?
What is flat life like?
Can you keep in touch with your house parents and social worker?

These were questions they admittedly struggled to answer. A group, they argued, would provide an opportunity to bring together young people who had recently left children's homes, and who were coping with the challenges of independent living, to share their experiences with those young people who were about to leave care.

Ad-Lib meetings

The first meeting was held in the cellar of a local children's home in January 1973, and the first task was to find a name for the group. But that was quickly resolved. One of the young people suggested calling the group *Ad-Lib*, short for both ad-libbing and adolescent liberation! All agreed it was '*a brilliant idea*' and it was unanimously adopted by the group.

Following the inaugural gathering, a group of 15 young people, who became known locally as *Ad-Libbers*, and four adults, who were committed to this new group work approach, but who had no social work responsibilities in relation to the individual members of the group, began to meet regularly. As well as the difficulties faced by

CHAPTER ONE

Beginning Ad-Lib

The idea of starting a group for young people in care came from two social workers, Ruth and Charlotte. They were influenced by the sort of questions put to them by young people in care when they talked to them individually. They were asked:

What is it like leaving care?

Do you have to go into lodgings?

What is flat life like?

Can you keep in touch with your house parents or social worker?

What is fostering like?

To answer these and other similar questions, Ruth and Charlotte would individually ask other young people who had recently left care and were living in lodgings or flats. If there were a group for young people it would encourage the sharing of ideas not only about the question of leaving care but about other things as well. Young people could talk to each other about being in care.

The idea was discussed within the area office and a paper outlining the scheme was prepared for the Director of Social Services and other members of management. Fortunately, a third social worker who was committed to the scheme at this stage, was based in central office and was able to drop some gentle hints! The idea received support from management and a small steering group of six people was set up within the division. The paper overleaf was then circulated to social service staff.

- 5 -

From Ad-Lib In Care Group Full Story, 1977[5]

young people leaving children's homes and moving to independence, as initially planned, a wide range of topics were aired and shared in the group during its first two years. These reflected some deeply held concerns for group members.

They included:

- young people's first memories of coming into care;
- how members of the public saw young people living in children's homes;
- the different types of punishments young people received in care and the reasons for them;
- how being in care affected their lives at school;
- the difficulties in bringing their friends back to their children's homes, and;
- the range of problems they experienced by living apart from their parents.

But there was a lot more to the *Ad-Lib* meeting than talking about topics. As many of the young people had to come from a distance to attend the group, transport was arranged by the adult members. This was the starting point for young people and adults to get to know each other better. It meant that the young people were not coming alone to the larger group. The informal arrival time lasted about ten minutes so that 'small talk' and catching up on news could happen

This was followed by the discussion time. A young person would usually chair the meeting and with two or three other young people start the ball rolling, often with plenty of wit and humour. At one group meeting, when the topic being discussed was '*how outsiders see young people in care*', a young man living in a large children's home recalled that when he went to the local fish and chip shop for the first time, and ordered 15 portions of fish and chips,, the chippy man smiled, winked and said: '*what does your old man do in his spare time then?*' The humour helped the group to relax, and for some of the new members, to laugh or smile was their main bond during their first couple of meetings. The discussion was also helped by the adults knowing the young people and being able to get them talking. After the discussion there was a break for records and grub, and a time arranged for the editorial *Ad-Lib Magazine* group to meet, before the lift home. Taken together, the different parts of the *Ad-Lib* meeting, the transporting, the arriving, the discussion, the break and going home, all contributed to the making of the group.

The *Ad-Lib* magazine was prepared by young people after each meeting, made up of contributions from the group. Its contents reflected the main points arising from the topics discussed, as well as poems, cartoons and jokes. It was distributed to all the local children's homes and social work offices in Leeds, and in this way the views of the *Ad Libbers* were to reach a far wider audience than the group itself. Its wide circulation also led to young people being invited to talk to residential workers, foster carers and students.

Ad-Lib changing things

The *Ad-Lib* group did a lot of talking and writing but it also wanted to change some of the things that young people had become more aware of in their group meetings.

First of all, young people were very angry about not being able to take money to pay for their school dinners. A 'special arrangement' between the Education and Social Services Departments meant that they were known as the 'welfare cases' in school. They were to remain seated whilst their class mates queued up to pay their dinner money. At the beginning of 1973 the *Ad-Libbers* wrote to the Director of Social Services:

'Everyone was in complete agreement that the present system of children from children's homes being singled out as having their dinner money paid directly from the Corporation was degrading and embarrassing. It was unanimously agreed that you be asked by this group to change the policy and allow all children to take their own dinner money weekly as other children do.'

The letter from the group brought about a swift change of policy, and *Ad-Lib's* first success. On 20 March 1973, the director responded:

'I have now received the 'go-ahead' from the City Treasurer to alter the system and that very shortly house parents will be able to make the necessary arrangements for you to take your dinner money with you to school.'

Second, the *Ad-Lib* group campaigned for young people living in care to be given money to buy their clothes. Again, they just wanted to be treated like other young people, by having cash and a choice of what to wear. But by another 'special arrangement' known as the 'clothing order book system', the Social Services Department had negotiated discounts with a couple of shops in Leeds for young people, including teenagers up to 18 years of age, to obtain clothing without payment. All that was required by this arrangement was for a member of staff from the children's home to accompany the young person to a listed shop, allow them to choose their clothing, and then conduct a paper transaction with the store supervisor. Well that is how it was seen by the department. The view from below was a little different:

'Waiting around for supervisors to be found and forms to be signed is tedious and very frustrating. The public stare inquisitively, looking disgusted, with the glint of accusation in their eyes, as if classifying us as shoplifters.'

'Money is better to use as nobody knows you come from a home. If we don't use money how can we lead a normal life, like all other kids, and when we are 18 we won't have a mind to shop for ourselves? We shouldn't feel we are the odd ones out.'

Once again, the *Ad-Libbers* decided to write to the Director of Social Services:

'At our last meeting there was a good deal of discussion about the buying of clothes on orders. Several young people pointed out that many shops won't accept the department's orders and that cheaper clothing, e.g. from the market, cannot be bought. We decided to write and ask whether it would be possible for us to have money available with which to buy clothes.'

The letter was sent to the director on 23 July 1973 but progress was to be very slow. In his initial response he wrote *'I take your point about 'shopping around.' One of the difficulties is the amount of loose cash which will have to be available.'* It was eventually agreed, in June 1974, nearly a year later, to launch a pilot scheme in two Leeds children's homes. But even following this trial period there was to be no outright ban in Leeds. It was to be left to the discretion of the manager of each children's home whether or not they used the clothing order book. This, as will be revealed later, proved to be the beginning of what was to become a long national campaign to *'Ban the Book.'*

These two 'special arrangements' stigmatised young people living in children's homes, making them feel *'singled out'* and bad about themselves. Such arrangements could be dismissed as purely 'administrative matters' and of little consequence to the lives of young people in care, but this logic would be mistaken. For these young people 'administrative arrangements' more than mattered, they shaped their lives. Their existence could only add to the deep rooted stigma experienced by those young people living apart from their families. In schools, neighbourhoods and all forms of media, 'the ideal family' loomed large. For those living in children's homes, their sense of loss and of being different was deeply felt.

As one young person wrote for the *Ad-Lib Mag*:

Unloved is to miss the love
that all parents should give
Yet they cast you aside
Put you out of their minds
They put you in care
There is no love there

Another young person from the group wrote about her feelings of rejection by her parents:

They can be so thoughtless and careless
of what they say
Yet we're the ones they hurt
by misunderstanding us in this
time of need when love could help us
We're the ones that are vulnerable
We need their love
But they won't change
They don't want to know
They haven't the time
They don't want to understand

As well as *'the inquisitive stare'* and the *'glint of accusation'*, young people felt in using order books to 'buy' their clothes, such 'special arrangements' incorporated a denial of choice and thus restricted the opportunity for young people to learn and do things for themselves. They were also highly insensitive to the way the disrupted family lives of young people in care had undermined their self esteem. What these young people needed were policies and practices to help them rebuild their confidence rather than further damage it.

Ad-Libber's views

But many of the practices at that time denied young people in care power and control over their lives, as captured by the voices of those who attended the *Ad-Lib* group.

'My first experience of being in care was as we waved good-bye to my grandma, not knowing or understanding what was happening. Tears filled my eyes. We hugged our big bag of clothes, being nothing but rags, and watched grandma crying.'

'We first went for a medical but I can't remember much of that. We were then, taken to our new home. At the time we didn't know we would never live with mum or dad again. No, we didn't know we were starting a new life.'

The important decisions about young people's lives were made at meetings called 'reviews,' although at that time young people had no legal right to attend.

'I would like to go to my own review to see what they said, and maybe tell them how I feel about what they said.'

'Reviews, they should not be like a secret, behind closed doors, where there is some people who know you and some people who are strangers, talking about you. You should be allowed to be in the review if you want to, and speak how you feel.'

Reviews were seen as powerful arenas by young people. But as they were not always informed about them, present at them, or prepared for them, this meant that they were sometimes feared by young people.

'I don't think you should be at your review because there may be things that will hurt your feelings. I don't think you should go because you don't know what you are walking into.'

Neither did young people have any right to see their own files - the official record of their life in care. These often remained locked up in filing cabinets.

'I would like to see my own file so that I would know exactly what happened to my family and why I was put in a home.'

'Yes, I would like to see my file to know what people think and say about you.'

'In care there are a lot of truths that you don't get to know about because you are too young or not able to understand, or just simply not told.'

As detailed above, the members of *Ad-Lib* also spoke and wrote of their feelings about their parents, their sadness, and their experience of pain and rejection which they brought with them into their children's homes. But young people didn't always experience or see children's homes or foster care as an alternative or replacement 'family'.

'I don't like the insecurity of never being able to call your home your own or the way you have to adjust your lives to suit complete strangers and not seeing your own family.'

'I dislike the way you have to ask permission from both foster parents and social worker before you are allowed to go away with a friend and her family or stay at a friend's home overnight.'

'To threaten to move a child from their home is very wrong because the child will never feel secure and loved if they are moved from place to place.'

'There is no privacy in my children's home.'

'Why do I have to call staff girls a couple of years older than myself Auntie? It's stupid.'

'Whilst I was there, in foster care, I held myself in so much that I hardly ever felt able to release the built up tension. This was because there I was, the charity girl. Always to be reminded of my good fortune and ingratitude. Maybe foster parents do this for social status - Christian Act. How kind they are - but are they? Don't they realise the damage they can do? Selfish. They play and use us for their goodness. I could never be myself there. They only knew the nice me, a one sided personality caged in respect and expected gratitude.'

Adding up *Ad-Lib*

During its first two years, young people found the *Ad-Lib* group helpful to them in a number of ways. This included meeting and making new friends with other young people in care and gaining confidence. '*It has helped the quiet ones come forward*' one young person remarked. It gave young people an opportunity to explore sometimes '*unspoken areas about care*' and growing up in care. It also assisted young people in learning about and planning for different types of care. Through its meetings, its *Ad-Lib Mag* and the talks young people gave to 'outsiders', the *Ad-Lib* group also helped the adult members, other social service workers and people outside of the care system to become more aware of, and sensitive to, how young people experienced their care. This led to more awareness of how young people were stigmatised by 'special arrangements' for school dinners and buying clothes, as well as some success by the group in changing policy.

The words of the *Ad-Libbers* also tell us about what care was like during the early 1970's. It was a care in part still touched by the long shadows of the poor law and charity. The administrative 'special arrangements' were highly insensitive to the needs of young people in care and were experienced by them as stigmatising and controlling. This was reinforced by their general lack of involvement in decisions that shaped their lives – including what was happening to them when they were taken into care, and their lives in care, including their reviews and access to their personal files. It was also a care that was still desperately trying to recreate the idea of 'the family' in children's homes whilst at the same time being subject to the authority of the bureaucratic parent.

Against the wider changes outlined at the beginning of this chapter, including the challenges to traditional social work ideas and practice, and the growing recognition of the 'rights' of disadvantaged groups, the Leeds *Ad-Lib* group pioneered a different approach and a way of responding to young people in care. But between 1973, when *Ad-Lib* began, and 1975, this remained a very local initiative. It was not known whether young people living in care elsewhere shared their experiences. The *Who Cares?* project changed all that.

Chapter 3

Who Cares?
'Spreading the word'

'Before we came to Who Cares? many of us thought it was going to be a day out, a skive off school or a con. But it wasn't. For the first time in my life people were listening to us and wanting to learn how we saw things.'

(Young person attending Who Cares? day conference in 1975)

'Some kids who wet the bed are made to sleep in it all night, then next night they make them sleep on the floor without any blankets.'

(Young person, Who Cares? Young people in care speak out, 1977)

Who Cares? - setting the scene

In June 1975 the National Children's Bureau organised a one-day conference and invited young people living in children's homes run by all local authorities and child care voluntary organisations across England and Wales. Nothing like this had happened before, a national gathering of 'troubled and troublesome' children. How could such an idea be seriously entertained?

This initiative was partly a response by the Bureau to find out the views of young people *themselves* about their lives in care which in the main had been ignored by policy makers, practitioners and researchers. The Leeds *Ad-Lib* group was, as yet, an exception. The Bureau also had concerns about the growth in the use of residential child care from the mid-1960's, including assessment centres, large children's homes and residential schools, and in particular, about whether these institutions could meet young people's emotional, educational and social needs.[6]

They were not alone in voicing their concerns. By the launch of their conference in 1975 residential care was widely criticised. The earlier 1960's classical institutional critiques, such as Goffman's *Asylums*, captured the dehumanising characteristics of what he described as *'forcing houses for changing persons,'* and connected with the growing popularity of community care.[7] The message was clear. The place for vulnerable people should be in the family and neighbourhood not in large segregated institutions. A rare anti-institutional, pro-community, academic and political consensus prevailed.

More specifically, in relation to child care, by 1975, the findings from *Children Who Wait* - Rowe and Lambert's 1973 seminal study highlighting the planning blight of children in long term care - had been taken on board by government.[8] This study had powerfully described the plight of those young people emotionally adrift in children's homes with little or no parental contact, but also with no plans for family rehabilitation, adoption or placement within a foster family. The study led directly to the rise of 'permanency planning.' This meant moving a child as soon as possible out of temporary care and returning them to their family or a permanent alternative such as adoption or long term fostering. The government's commitment to facilitate these changes was reflected in the provisions of the Children Act 1975, including extending the grounds for local authorities to assume parental rights, and making adoption easier through 'freeing for adoption' and the introduction of custodianship orders.

The Act also, for the first time, placed a duty on local authorities '*to ascertain as far as is practicable the wishes and feelings of the child and give due consideration to them, having regard to his age and understanding.*' This was to prove a legal landmark for the rights movement for young people in care but not at this point in time. As will be discussed later, it wasn't until this duty was consolidated in the Child Care Act 1980 that it assumed this significance. Its inclusion in the 1975 Act was primarily in response to the death of Maria Colwell at the hands of her stepfather, having been returned from a settled and loving foster care placement. The inquiry into her death highlighted the failure of social workers to take into account her views.[9] In this context, the duty to ascertain '*wishes and feelings*' was seen in practice as related to listening to the views of children involved in child protection cases about who they wanted to live with, as distinct from consulting young people in care about their lives – although it did promote the legal framework for the latter.

Those who opposed the permanency movement, seeing it as an attack on poor families, by legalising separation from their children, advocated far greater support for families in the community to prevent their children coming into care in the first place. They were also strongly opposed to the placement of children in residential care. This perspective gave birth to the Family Rights Group in 1975. Residential care was also rejected by many youth justice workers who at that time saw their mission as diverting young people from entering care and custody in the first place, through the provision of community-based programmes.

It was in this negative context surrounding residential child care that the National Children's Bureau set out to explore the views of young people living in children's homes, and find out whether they echoed wider concerns about institutional life. The Bureau was well placed to organise such an event. They already had experience of involving, and working with, local school children in a vanguard participatory project - which was viewed as very progressive at that time.

Also, Mia Kellmer Pringle, the Bureau's director, led from the front. Her own childhood suffering at the hands of the Nazis who had murdered her father, and forced her as a teenager and her mother to flee their home to become Jewish refugees in England, led to her commitment and belief in listening to, and learning from, children. A close colleague suggested that although Mia was a psychologist she mistrusted professionals and believed children knew better than adults.[10] It was children who carried the messages of pain and suffering. Mia, herself, had been a victim of 'adult society' - she had seen children being rounded up by the Nazis. The professional task was to understand and respond to the messages from children in any way they could. Listening to them was the starting point.

Who Cares? Young People in Care Speak Out

One hundred young people between the ages of 12 and 16, all living in children's homes, came along to the *Who Cares?* day conference in June 1975. Assisted by four adults who themselves had grown up in care, they spoke, many for the first time, freely and openly about their experiences.

'Before we came to Who Cares? many of us thought it was going to be a day out, a skive off school or a con. But it wasn't. For the first time in my life people were there listening to us and wanting to learn how we saw things.'

These young people voiced their hopes and aspirations as well as their anger and frustrations. So much came out of the day that the young people wanted to meet again and prepare a statement of their views for the 'outside' world. In July 1975, a month after the conference, 16 young people met and called themselves the *Who Cares? Young People's Working Group*. At the first of their meetings, the eight adults who helped organise the June event, including the four adults whom had grown up in care, were co-opted on to the group by the young people. Their aspirations at the first meeting were high. Such was the enthusiasm and momentum from the original day that the group's suggestion to write a book, rather than prepare a 'mere statement' was unanimously adopted.

Group members, supported by the Bureau, met together for one day every six weeks between July 1975 and February 1977. Their taped conversations, which were read, discussed and agreed by the young people, became the book, *Who Cares? Young People In Care Speak Out.*[11] It was published in September 1977 and was headline news for the day! The national media including television, radio and newspapers, provided extensive coverage. But by the following day it had disappeared from the popular news agenda. More enduring, however, were the issues raised by the young people, some resonating with those raised by the Leeds *Ad-Lib* group.

To begin with young people wrote about the stigma of care, but not so much the specific policies and practices, more the personal consequences - the depth of guilt felt by young people.

'When I first went to my school there was some money being pinched and I felt so guilty because I knew I was from a children's home and I felt I was picked on, and I knew it wasn't me.'

'People think that if you're in care you must have done something wrong. I met a girl and I wouldn't tell her I came from a children's home but she found out. I was so embarrassed. I was ashamed.'

'My house-father once said to me: "If you don't tell anyone you're in a home, then I won't."'

The attitudes of teachers could also make school a very difficult experience for young people living in children's homes.

'When I went to school there was a music teacher and the least little thing I used to do wrong he'd say, "you're all the bloody same you lot."'

But neither did these young people want to be singled out by misguided sympathy.

'And yet the one thing I can't stand is people feeling sorry for us. That's worse than them thinking we're just a lot of yobbos.'

At the time when the *Who Cares?* day conference was held in June 1975 there was very little public awareness about why young people came into care, or about their lives in children's homes. There was a widespread misconception that they it was their fault, that they were blameworthy.

'People think that if you're in care you must have done something wrong. The first question they ask is: "What did you do?"'

'I mean I always used to be threatened with being put away in a home where they're always nasty to you. That's the general impression that everybody outside has.'

'We want the average person to find out that children in care aren't something that you avoid like the plague.'

Another issue, and one discussed by the Leeds *Ad-Libbers* was whether children's homes were also seen by young people attending the *Who Cares?* conference, as what social workers often referred to as their 'substitute family'.

'However well you get on with your house parents, when our mum comes down it's a real treat to call somebody mum.'

'There are times when I feel like lashing out at someone - even my best mate - just because I miss a family atmosphere and the feeling that someone really cares for me and loves me.'

'At first when I was put in a home, it didn't affect me so much but after a while I wanted love, and I wanted my mother mainly. And she wasn't there. And I used to be desperate all the time for my mother and she'd never turn up. A few years later, I realised that she wasn't going to come and I wasn't going to get the love because there was too many children for the staff to pinpoint one to care about.'

Also, like the members of the *Ad-Lib* group, the young people recognised the falseness of calling staff 'mum', 'dad', 'aunt' or 'uncle'.

'The little ones call them 'mummy' or 'daddy' because they don't know better. But I just can't because they aren't. How'd you think my mum'd feel if she heard me calling them 'mum''

But these young people also recognised that caring for them was a job, and an important one that needed trained staff.

'It's a job. It's not just 'looking after kids.' A lot of kids when they come into care really freak out. I mean they're pretty mixed up. Some kids have had a rough time at home, a really rotten time. But it's a job and staff get paid for it and they're there to set us an example and show us they care and help us sort out our problems.'

The spoken and written words of the *Who Cares?* young people in 1977, echoed in many ways the ambiguous identity of care voiced by members of the *Ad-Lib* group. What the meaning of care was to these young people was unattainable parental expectations, but neither was there an alternative professional vision. Care was failing many of them both as a substitute and professional parent.

Those attending *Who Cares?* also spoke of the disruption they experienced. Many had moved frequently in their short lives - from children's homes to foster care, returning to their family for short periods before returning to care again.

'It's the coming and going that hurts. The first time you move to another place it hurts bad so you build up a shell but one day the shell cracks.'

'I want to know where I'm going to be living and what's going to happen to me. I've been in so many places.'

One young person said that the most hurtful thing about care was the '*chopping and changing*'. For other young people this was compounded by changing social workers, residential workers and the shift system in children's homes.

'My brother and I have had more social workers than I can remember. They'd see us once and then disappear for six months, then we'd have a new one. And it's been going on all the time, they've been leaving or they've been going ill. And if that's happening all the time, I don't see how they can help you.'

'There's the day staff and the night staff and you never know who's on. And when staff leave, we can be the last people to know.'

'It's a job…it's not just looking after kids'

The disruption and instability described by those young people attending *Who Cares?* raised fundamental questions about the rationale of the care system at that time. If society had judged the parents of these children unfit to care for them, and thus unable to provide for their emotional security, how well were their carers, as 'substitute parents' meeting their needs? If they were unable to give them a stable foundation, as was the situation for many of these young people by 1977, what was the purpose of them being in care at all?

These young people's voices and words also raised very disturbing questions about the quality of life in some children's homes at that time, including the use of physical punishment.

'Some kids who wet the bed are made to sleep in it all night, then next night they make them sleep on the floor without any blankets.'

'When I first went to this children's home, if you did wrong, the housefather would grab hold of you and take you up to the bedroom and start beating you about, and he did this to me once. He threw me over the bed and he got hold of my brother and just threw him straight into the washing basin. And he went downstairs and didn't do a thing about it, just left him up there, cut all over his face.'

The use of physical punishment was so much the norm that it was sometimes accepted as 'natural' by young people.

'When you're in care, you have to be careful - you never let 'them' know what you really care about. Because if they find out they'll use it against you. Like losing your privileges, not letting you home to see your folks. Before I came to Who Cares? I thought it was all right for the staff to knock us about. It's happened in so many places I've been in.'

'Well, I don't think that there should be a rule against staff hitting. I have always been hit round the face by a member of staff and it's done me some good.'

Many of these young people had experienced physical violence and emotional abuse in their own families, and this contributed in no small way to them being taken in to care in the first place. It is cruelly ironic then that they were also to suffer such abuses at the hands of their 'carers'. Not only that, these revelations, although published in *Who Cares? Young People in Care Speak Out* and receiving widespread publicity at that time, didn't generate the public, political and professional outcry that led to government action 20 years later. If they had sparked such a reaction at that time who knows how many more children and young people would have been safeguarded. Which raises the question: why was there so little response at that time? This is a question I will return to in the concluding chapter.

The young people attending *Who Cares?* also raised questions about 'not knowing' and 'not being involved' in very important decisions and processes which influenced their lives.

'When you're small you're just taken away from the family and nobody tells you why and you think it's your fault. I think little 'uns should be told why they're being taken into care.'

'They've got an order on me and I'm in till I'm 18. Nobody's ever told me before you could get the order changed if you're able to go home or look after yourself.'

'I've never been to my review. I asked, but they won't let me.'

The *Who Cares?* young people were also often upset at the way their reviews were carried out when they were invited to attend.

'To me a review is a very private part of our life. When you walk in, you see many strange faces, people you don't know, people who know all about you but you know nothing about them.'

Finally, these young people raised questions about when care ends, about the connection between their lives in care and reaching eighteen (although many left at just 16 or 17), and leaving care to live independently.

'I want to get out but then I don't want to because I don't have anybody outside.'

'The thing about being in care is there's no way you can grow up, you are a child until you're 18 and really you're not.'

'If you live with your parents you have a choice whether you leave home or not. In care you get kicked out, you don't feel you belong there once you have left'.

'They do everything for you; I don't really know how to look after myself.'

Who Cares? Young People in Care Speak Out also contained the first published *Charter of Rights for Young People In Care* and the first published programme of *The Things We Want To Change*, both prepared by young people themselves.

Charter of Rights for Young People In Care

We have drawn up this charter for 'young people' because we feel it is the responsibility of the residential worker and social worker to make sure that younger kids get a good deal.

1. *The right to be accepted as an individual member of society. Also the right to be treated with the same respect given to any other valid member of the human race.*

2. *The right to know who we are. To know our parents and brothers and sisters. To have factual information about our family origins and background.*

3. *The right to be able to make our own decisions and to have real influence over those decisions we are considered too thick to participate in.*

4. *The right to privacy. We understand that in care it is not always possible to choose who we are going to live and share our lives with. But we are still human beings and are still entitled to the essential amount of privacy needed before cracking up.*

5. *The right to be given an insight into the use of money by handling it, using it and paying the consequences if we misuse it, e.g. being given the money in our hand to buy the clothes our clothing allowance will allow.*

6. *The right to choose who will represent us whether it be legally or otherwise, e.g. social workers. Also the right to choose those whom we wish to confide in.*

7. *Finally, the right to be as much a part of society as the next person and not to be labelled in any way. In short, to live.*

These rights can be interpreted how you like. But don't misuse them or distort them for your own devices.

'The right to be accepted as an individual member of society'

The Things We Want To Change

1. *Give us a chance to find a voice and to speak and mix with ordinary people so that public attitudes about care can be changed for the better. Set up Who Cares? groups throughout the country.*

2. *Give all young people in care a chance to attend their own six-monthly review. Give us a say in who attends, besides the social worker, their boss and the people we live with. Younger children need someone to speak for them. Learn how to talk with us and learn how to listen. Give all children in care a voice in their life.*

3. *Do away with the order book and special voucher scheme for buying our clothing. It will save money if we are allowed to shop in ordinary stores - not just the most expensive ones. Do away with special tokens for paying for our school dinners.*

4. *Help the residential and field social workers to find ways of working more closely together than they do at present. They should stop pulling in opposite directions, against the children.*

5. *Bring pocket money and clothing allowance into line nationally so that most children of the same age get roughly the same allowance. Children should know how much the allowance is and what it is expected to cover.*

6. *Help us to have a realistic approach to sex education and personal relationships. Enable us to learn how to look after ourselves - not suddenly at 18 expect us to know all the things we've never had a chance to learn.*

7. *Help us sort out our education while we're young. A lot of us have missed out on our schooling through being in care and moving from place to place.*

8. *Make sure every young person in care really understands their situation, why they cannot live with their family. Give us factual information - a booklet or leaflet - to explain care and the law that affects us. When we leave care, make sure we know what help we can reasonably ask for and expect to get.*

9. *Ask local authorities to decide whether or not corporal punishment is allowed in their children's homes. Children in care should know what the ruling is and who they can turn to for help if they think they are being ill-treated. This is delicate but it can be done.*

10. *Find ways of letting us help children younger than ourselves. Give us something to work for while we are in care.*

These two documents were a watershed in relation to the emerging rights movement for young people in care. For the first time in the history of child welfare a *Charter of Rights* and a programme of *The Things We Want to Change* had been prepared, agreed and written by young people themselves. Also, the wide publicity afforded to *Who Cares? Young People in Care Speak Out*, especially in reaching those working in child care, meant that a new idea, the 'rights of young people in care' could begin to claim a space in social work's conceptual landscape. Their *Charter of Rights* articulated four main different kinds of rights.

First of all, the right to equality: young people in care wanted to be treated equally – *'with the same respect'* and *'be as much a part of society'* – as other young people, and not be discriminated against by virtue of being in care. As the experience of members of the Leeds *Ad-Lib* group and *Who Cares?* showed, many young people living in children's homes felt discriminated against: for example, in not being given money to pay for their school dinners, and having to use order books to buy clothes, as well as the attitudes towards them at school. In these ways, their experiences reflected the historical experience of other disadvantaged groups. As one young person commented, *'being in care you feel you've got a cross on your back. You feel marked'*.

Second, the right to be informed about their lives: young people wanted *'to know who we are'*. There were many gaps in the life stories of young people. They wanted the right to know all about their lives in care, including their family background, the reasons for coming into care, and what happened to them in care and the reasons why. They wanted a coherent story of their lives, not least to help them understand their background and provide them with an emotional platform for making sense of their lives and moving on.

Third, young people wanted the right to participate in decision making. As described above, many of the young people who attended the *Who Cares?* events felt excluded from important decisions that affected their lives. They wanted to have *'a real influence over those decisions,'* including, everyday decisions, attendance at their reviews, the right to use money, as well as '*to choose who will represent us*'.

Fourth, young people wanted the right to privacy. It is very difficult for those living in children's homes to have a private life, or their own personal space free from staff intrusion or other young people. But the members of the *Who Cares? Action Group* felt very strongly that they should have this right – '*we are still human beings*'.

Also, contained within *The Things We Want to Change* were specific policy and practice demands linked to the framework of rights. Young people wanted to attend their reviews; to have more and better quality information, especially in booklets or leaflets; and to be rid of stigmatising practices such as clothing order books and special tokens for school dinners. They also wanted the introduction of a national age-related system of pocket money and clothing allowances, to reduce the gross inequalities in the payments made by different local authorities.

But their programme for change also contained other important ideas. Young people wanted a person to '*turn to for help if they think they are being ill-treated,*' in other words, a complaints procedure. Who knows, if that suggestion had been acted upon in 1977 it may have prevented the abuse and suffering of many young people. They also wanted far more preparation for leaving care, '*not suddenly at 18,*' the expectation of instant adulthood. They suggested that this could include a role for 'older' young people in care to assist younger ones – '*find ways of letting us help children younger than ourselves*' - or the idea of peer mentoring, way ahead of its time! Young people wanted more help with education, less disruption in their lives, and for social workers and residential staff to work together more closely -'*stop pulling in opposite directions.*' Finally, they wanted to change public attitudes about care - '*to speak and mix with ordinary people,*' - by setting up *Who Cares?* groups throughout the country. No mean challenge - but one they were up for!

Chapter 4

Who cares wins?

'Great! I said to myself, something I have always wanted to do, express my thoughts and opinions about living in care.'

(Young person attending the Yorkshire group, November 1977)

'Being 15 and in care, I have had to suffer public baths. I don't mean swimming baths, I mean having to bath and shower in front of staff of 22 years of age – both men and women......I found this a distressing situation......should this be allowed?'

(Young man writing in Who Cares? News, 1979)

Involving young people in Who Cares?

The young people who formed the original *Who Cares?* group felt very strongly that other young people living in care in different parts of the country, should be given the same opportunity to meet and talk about their lives with interested adults. The success of *Who Cares?* led the National Children's Bureau to secure further funding to set up four regional groups. These were held between April 1977 and January 1978 in inner London and the Home Counties (both groups meeting in London), in the Midlands which met in Birmingham and in Yorkshire which met in Leeds.

The Bureau's two development workers identified the purpose of the new groups as threefold: *first of all, to replicate the original Who Cares? national event by engaging young people living in children's homes in a dialogue with adults about their experiences of care; second, for each group to agree a specified task, to be completed during the life of the group; and third, to find ways to bring their group's views and concerns to a wider public, in particular, by influencing those responsible for shaping their lives, including teachers, local councillors, and social work staff.*[12]

The four new groups were launched in a similar way to the original *Who Cares?* national event. A day conference was held in each of the regions to which all young people over the age of 12 living in children's homes were invited, accompanied by their 'carers', their house parents or social workers. A small number of adults, selected and prepared by the Bureau, led the event. At the end of the day those young people wishing to take things further were given the chance to join an ongoing regional group.

A young person who attended the Yorkshire *Who Cares?* launch wrote:[13]

'Great! I said to myself, something I have always wanted to do, express my thoughts and opinions about living in care. So on Saturday 26 November 1977, I, with two other children from the home, together with our officer in charge and senior house mother, went to the meeting at Leeds University.

We arrived there somewhat uncertain. However, after being given information, coffee and biscuits we were split up into two groups, all social workers and house parents in one group and the children in care in another group, and then we split into smaller groups. In our group we talked about pocket money, clothing allowances, reviews, punishments, how being in care affects you in school and in the neighbourhood, smoking in care and bedtimes.

The young people all met again in one large group and were asked, 'Do we want the adults to come in our group in the second half of the day?' Most of us voted that they should come in, so after lunch we all met together. This to me was the most important part of the day, for now we could see both points of view.

Some of the questions asked by us, children in care, were: why should we call the staff 'sir' or 'miss' or 'auntie' or 'uncle', why couldn't we just call them Joe, Jenny, Steve or Jack, in other words by their first names? Other children asked: why was their pocket money different from that of somebody the same age in care elsewhere?

This question and answer time went on for about one hour and then we were asked, if anybody would be interested in taking things further, they would be given the chance to join a working party of young people in care beginning in January and meeting at regular intervals.'

The regional groups met every four or five weeks and their membership settled down to between ten and 20 young people and seven adults. As with the original *Who Cares?* day and the regional launch events, the adults were to play a key role in enabling young people to participate in the groups. This meant that they were 'independent' adults. None of them had any supervisory or direct caring role in respect of the young people attending the groups. But what was important was that they were able to identify with the group's aims and philosophy: to encourage young people to talk, to help all young people in the group to express themselves, and to be able to listen to their views. No social work jargon - and there was a lot about - was permitted!

Many of the issues raised by young people in the regional groups echoed those from the original *Who Cares?* day, outlined in chapter 3. Young people living in children's homes in different areas of England shared many common experiences: their lack of knowledge about their own lives and about the care system generally; their lack of power and control over their lives; their fears and worries about leaving care and coping with life after care; and their wish - too often thwarted by movement, disruption and staff turnover - for a stable trusting adult in their lives.

Also, the agenda of these new groups included attempts to bring about change by influencing those responsible for their lives. To achieve this at the local level the groups held 'open days' to which social workers, teachers, magistrates, residential workers and local councillors were invited. In addition, one of the groups, located within a single local authority, met with the local Director of Social Services and held regular meetings, parallel to the young people's group, between the adult group leaders and field, residential and managerial social work staff.

Who Cares? News

Representatives from the regional groups also came together for a number of joint activities and in doing so began to lay the organisational foundations of the *Who Cares?* movement. These activities included the publication of *Who Cares News*, the first national magazine for young people in care, launched in the spring of 1978. The editorial board was made up of 11 young people from the regional groups who met regularly at the National Children's Bureau in London, supported by a member of their staff. They decided which articles to include, wrote the editorial column for each edition, and sought out new copy when needed from the regional groups.

Five issues were produced during the life span of the regional groups, from the spring of 1978 to the summer 1979. This included 500 copies of the first issue and, because of demand, 1,000 copies of the other four issues. In addition, the magazine was widely circulated among both young people living in children's homes and adult carers. Also, 'to spread the word,' the Bureau re-printed the first four editions in its own journal *Concern* with a circulation of 5,000 subscribers, including those working in education, health, youth work and children's social care.[14] This was a significant landmark in the history of the movement. It meant that, for the first time, the views and opinions of young people living in children's homes were being communicated to a far wider professional audience than had been the case to date.

The regional groups, as suggested earlier, validated many of the issues raised by the original *Who Cares?* group. This was reflected in the contents of *Who Cares News*, in the articles written by young people on topics such as reviews, teachers, privacy, punishments and leaving care.[15] But new topics were also introduced and old ones expressed more creatively. In the launch edition, the issue of '*colour prejudice*' was raised for the first time in the '*grapevine column*' of the magazine.

There's a Bloke

'There's a bloke in one of our council homes and I don't know what he is doing there. He's the governor and he is colour prejudice against anyone who isn't English. And people like that shouldn't be in a position like that. Because if you're in charge of kids, you take kids no matter what colour or nationality. People are people, no matter what. I just can't stand colour prejudice.'

In the same issue, a young man wrote about the lack of privacy in his children's home.

Who Cares about public baths?

'Being 15 and in care, I have had to suffer public baths. I don't mean swimming baths, I mean having to bath or shower in front of staff of 22 years of age - both men and women. Being a sexually aware normal 15-year old male, I found this a distressing situation, both for myself and the staff, especially when one of the staff called me 'darling' when she saw my naked body. Should this be allowed? Should young adolescents have to suffer this way? What are the staff getting out of it? I didn't like it.'

Some of the young people expressed their views in poetry. In the fourth issue one young man wrote about leaving care.

Constant years of tight held hand and dominant guidance,
Following bewildered on the red tape lead of Boroughs' policies,
Systematically filed - regularly tested.
Separated safely to a distant spot,
Suckling on the eager breast of care,
Sympathetically cuddled, caressed, enclosed.
To what end this mothering protection?
To produce a weak unprepared inexperienced child,
To face a hostile world.

Some of the topics raised in the original *Who Cares?* group were explored in more depth in the regional groups and this was also reflected in the contributions to *Who Cares News*. The Wakefield group, an off shoot from the Yorkshire group, wrote about reviews.

'Sometimes reviews are held when you are at school or work, so it is impossible to attend. This should be avoided. Sometimes it is difficult to understand what people are talking about. They should try to put things in a simple language. You should be given plenty of warning that a review is taking place. Sometimes we are only told on the morning of the review - or even after it has taken place! It would be useful if we knew which topics were to be discussed before the review so that we could decide whether or not we want to stay for all or just some of the review.'

'We feel that if things are difficult to accept or talk about they should still be discussed openly and to your face. We would like more say about who attends reviews. You ought to be able to choose whether or not your family attends. Sometimes you do not know who has come to your review. People should introduce themselves. To them you are just a name. They do not know you but they know things about you. Whatever is decided at a review should be explained clearly. You should be told what is to take place and when it will happen.'

Many young people from children's homes attending the regional *Who Cares?* felt unwanted by their family. But at the same time, care was unable to provide them with stability, as captured by this poem.

Who Cares?

We are the 'Who Cares'
I care
Do you care?
Mother doesn't care
Papa's on the dole
And nobody there

Pushed here
Pushed there
Pushed blooming everywhere
Different faces
Different graces
We try to keep up these speedy paces.

We feel we haven't got much say
Punishment most every day.

The Who Cares? action group

In addition to producing *Who Cares? News*, representatives from the regional groups also came together to make four video tapes. The topics chosen were review meetings, teachers and schools, discipline and punishment in children's homes, and coping with the challenges of leaving care and setting up home. They were made for the purpose of educating different professional audiences, including teachers, health workers and youth workers, about the experiences and views of young people living in children's homes.

Also, young people from the inner London regional group took part in two television programmes, *Kids United* for the peak viewing *World in Action* current affairs series, and BBC 2's *A Child's Place* series, to mark the International Year of the Child. Both programmes gave young people the chance to talk extensively about their lives in care and were very successful in reaching a far wider and more general public audience than hitherto.

The movement was also strengthened by two national events. The first of these, the *Who Cares? Jamboree*, was held on 8 July 1978 at the National Children's Bureau in London and attended by 120 young people's delegates and 20 adults. The young people came from the Bureau's four regional groups, as well as seven other local groups, most of which were off shoots from the regions. The Leeds

Ad-Lib group, the very first group, was still going strong and sent nine delegates to the jamboree day.

The day began with a '*Reports from the Groups*' session at which it became very evident from the outset that bringing about changes in policy and in practice and not just talking about 'the same old issues' was high on the agenda, particularly of those experienced young people who had been involved since the launch day of *Who Cares?* in 1975. They wanted *Who Cares?* to be more than just a 'talking shop'. Delegates' suggestions to bring about change included talking to the media in their local areas – '*as we, children in care, have nothing to lose, talking to the media might do a lot of good.*'

Some delegates also spoke of the difficulties faced by individual children and young people in making complaints to staff in their children's homes. They suggested that a *Who Cares?* group could provide a way to help young people voice their complaints. But, it was agreed that for this to work, the group would have to be recognised by local social service departments. Another suggestion was that there should be regular meetings of young people and staff in children's homes, to provide opportunities for young people to participate in making changes in the home in a mature and responsible way.

After lunch, young people participated in one of six action groups which they had selected when responding to their invitation. The topics chosen were: living in children's homes; preparing for leaving care; planning our lives; training for adults working with children in care; teachers and schools; and growing up black in care. Young people in the groups took responsibility for taking notes and for writing them up so a report could be produced.

In fact, the amount of material generated from the day, including feedback from the groups, as well as the commitment and impetus from those attending the jamboree to do something about the issues raised, led to the formation of the *Who Cares?* action group. Nineteen young people and ten adults were nominated by delegates to take further action on their behalf. The newly formed group was to meet at Ruskin College, Oxford, between 29 September and 1 October 1978, to carry out its action brief. The Ruskin weekend proved to be a watershed in the movement's history.

Prior to the Ruskin weekend it had been rumoured that the funding of the *Who Cares?* project was coming to an end: the substantial commitment by the National Children's Bureau in providing staffing and money to support national or local group meetings of young people would shortly cease. Confirmation of this bad news at the Ruskin College event left both the young people and adults from local groups feeling very angry. This was not just in response to the sudden notice given by the Bureau - somewhat ironic in view of the group's contribution in highlighting the lack of consultation in care. But it was also in the realisation that *Who Cares?* had no funding for the future, or formal organisation, in terms of a membership, officers, or elected committee, to provide for ongoing meetings and contact. Fortunately, it did have the *Who Cares?* action group.

As discussed above, the Ruskin weekend was planned '*to work towards action*' and delegates arrived at Ruskin with a commitment to '*do something*' to bring about change. A cocktail of anger, frustration and concern led to delegates agreeing policy recommendations, and to the preparation of articles and letters for the national press, journals and magazines and professional bodies and associations. This included letters on the use of clothing vouchers, the training of social workers and public attitudes to children in care. In respect of the latter, the *Who Cares?* action group decided to target the Daily Mirror. On 6 October 1978 it wrote to the editor:

Dear Editor

'Delinquents, orphans, poor deprived little children.'

'Isn't it good of the Social Services to provide them with all their needs?'

'Our taxes pay for their support.'

Here are just a few examples of the verbal attentions young people in care receive today – expressed with disgust, pity and objective charity.

I am writing on behalf of the Who Cares? action group, a group of young people set up for young people in care, about young people in care and run by young people in care, whose general outcry is – 'Please treat us like human beings.'

Being in care is not an easy ride. The pity we receive does not help us grow up to lead a positive adult life.

Delinquent is the wrong description for the total number of young people in care. There are many reasons for children being in care. Many are there through no fault of their own and it doesn't help being labelled as delinquent.

Finally, as for the needs we are provided with, these are just material goods. A child also has the need for love and affection, not just a warm bed and a record player.

*We have feelings too, just as ordinary human beings have. We want your concern
without your pity*

Yours faithfully

Young Person (aged 15, on behalf of the Who Cares? action group)

On 23 October 1978 the Daily Mirror responded with an article.[16]

Branded...the innocent kids

**Innocent children who are put into care because their parents can't look after
them claim that they are being treated like criminals**

*They say that they are branded in the same way as young offenders who live in
the same homes.*

*Now they have formed a 'union' – the Young People's Action Group – to fight for
their rights.*

*Representatives of the 60,000 non-offenders in council care explained yesterday
how they are always branded as delinquents.*

*THEY are punished at school if anything is stolen – because teachers
automatically blame them.*

*THEY face discrimination from their friends who think children in care
are offenders.*

*THEY never know whether to own up to living in a children's home when job
hunting – for they believe that bosses also turn their backs on them.'*

Who Cares? making a difference

The Ruskin weekend marked the end of the *Who Cares?* project, exposing its
organisational and campaigning weaknesses. Its sudden ending had failed to leave young
people with their own organisation. But never the less, a lot had still been achieved.

For the first time, the views of young people living in children's homes had
received widespread publicity. They had reached both the general public and a
range of different professional groups who worked with children and young people.
The public interest may have been short lived, not to be reawakened until the abuse

scandals in children's homes many years later. But the impact upon child welfare policy and practice of the new thinking about the rights of children and young people in care, as articulated in the Charter of Rights, was to become permanent. A new discourse had begun.

The Who Cares? project also led to the setting up of groups of young people in care in different areas of England and Wales. Like its predecessor, the Leeds *Ad-Lib* group, they provided a platform for the views and opinions of young people to be heard in their local area. In doing so they were able to bring about some changes locally, and help group members develop their confidence.

The views of young people who participated in *Who Cares?* both validated and extended many of the main themes identified by the *Ad-Lib* group concerning the identity of care during these years. Many of these young people experienced their 'care' as disruptive and controlling, excluding them from major decisions that affected them. It was a care that often failed to compensate them for the problems they had come into care with: neither, acting as a 'good parent' or offering them a positive alternative. And some young people were to suffer further abuse at the hands of their 'carers', although there seemed little public or professional will to do something about the plight of these young people.

However, it was the future of *Who Cares?* once the Bureau's project funding ended which concerned most delegates during the Ruskin weekend. Feelings of commitment and anger led experienced delegates to recognise the weaknesses and limitations of *Who Cares?* It was seen as a 'talking shop' raising expectations and then leading to frustration and a loss of interest. The same feelings united them in their call for an organisation that would bring local groups together and campaign around issues and policies.

Chapter 5

The National Association of Young People In Care (NAYPIC)
The early years 1979-1983

'The 30 June 1979 was a very historic date for young people in care. The setting up of NAYPIC meant that for the first time they had their own independent organisation to pursue their aims. It was an organisation they had created.'

NAYPIC: how it began

The unexpected death of *Who Cares?* shocked the young people who attended the Ruskin weekend. They felt very let down, even, to some degree, 'used' to serve the interests of a professionally led project. Also, at a more practical level, they had been given very little time to think about the future. But think about it they did. The *Who Cares?* action group was determined to build upon the commitment and momentum that had been generated. It was successful in securing a small grant from the Cadbury Trust to fund three national meetings of representatives of *Who Cares?* groups. At these meetings, held during April and May 1979, there was widespread support for the action group's proposals to set up a new independent organisation for young people in care. Progress was swift.

On the 30 June 1979 NAYPIC was launched at the Leeds University Adult Education Centre. At the inaugural meeting there were representatives from ten 'in care' groups: young people and adult members from Bradford, Coventry,

Hounslow, London, Leeds, the North East, Wakefield, Wandsworth, Westminster and Scotland attended the event. The constitution was approved and a management committee elected, consisting of young people representing all the local groups, and three co-opted adults. The aims of the new organisation as defined by the constitution were:

1. To improve conditions for children and young people in care;

2. To make information and advice available to young people in care;

3. To promote the views and opinions of young people in care; and

4. To help start, support and develop local groups.

Membership was to be open to *'anyone who is in care or has been in care in the past and other people voted in by a local group.'* Local groups could affiliate to NAYPIC and be entitled to have one representative on the management committee, *'which should be a young person in care.'* Also, by the constitution, co opted adult members were not to form more than one third of the management committee. At the inaugural meeting it was also agreed by the members that NAYPIC should pursue charitable status, essential if it was to secure funding in its own right as an organisation. There was also strong support for NAYPIC to publish its own newsletter, *NAYPIC News*, as well as launch a national campaign to *Ban the Book* - the much reviled clothing order book, still used by many young people to obtain their clothing

The 30 June 1979 was a historic date for young people in care. The setting up of NAYPIC meant that for the first time they had their own independent organisation to pursue their aims. It was an organisation they had created, unlike the professionally instigated and led *Who Cares?* project. But they owed a big debt to *Who Cares?*

By 1979 the idea of rights for children in care was gaining both professional and political ground. As discussed in chapter 3, in 1977 *Who Cares?* published the first *Charter of Rights for Young People in Care*. This represented a landmark, by challenging the way children and young people in care were understood by child care professionals. From that time onwards they were to be seen as having 'rights' as well as 'needs'. This shift towards rights was also reflected in wider debates in social work about the status that should be attached to the views of 'clients', especially adults, including their participation in decision making and their right to quality services, as well as to complain if they were not satisfied with the service they received. This new way of thinking also represented a serious challenge to the status of professionalism, especially the established view that the professional always 'knows what's best for you.'[17]

There were also new children's rights organisations. Justice for Children was founded in 1978 to advocate for greater protection of young people's rights in the juvenile justice system. This was not, as might be expected today, in response to their detention in custody, but to the indeterminate nature of welfare interventions, by the use of care orders that allowed social services to detain young people until they were 18 without legal redress to the courts.

In 1979, the Children's Legal Centre was set up '*to promote the recognition of children and young persons as individuals participating fully in all the decisions which affect their lives.*' This statement of purpose was by far the most radical perspective on children's rights to date in England. Children and young people were seen as having the same rights as adults: to '*participate fully in all decisions*' that shape their lives. More globally, 1979 was also the International Year of the Child, at the end of which Poland proposed the first United Nations Convention on the Rights of the Child – although it took another ten years to come to fruition!

Paradoxically, perhaps, the emergence of the 'New Right' and the election of the Thatcher government in May 1979 was fertile ground for consumerism in public services. In opposition, the Conservatives had attacked Labour's 'nanny state', a welfare state that they saw not only as bureaucratic and inefficient but also as over controlling of people's lives. The rise of consumer and rights groups - as long as the radical causes some of them espoused were not too closely examined - provided ammunition for the Conservative's attacks on Labour's state control: such groups were viewed as a progressive example of self-help, to be supported whilst in opposition and later when in power.

Finally, by way of context, in chapter 3, I described the Children Act 1975 as a legal landmark in respect of children's rights. It introduced new duties to '*ascertain the wishes and feelings*' of young people in adoption decisions and local authority care. The introduction of these consultative rights were important because for the first time in law the interests of the 'child' were disaggregated from the interests of 'the family'. The 1975 Act had also made provisions for the separate representation of children in court from their parents through the appointment of *Guardians ad Litem*, again recognising potential conflicts of interest for the first time in this setting. I also argued in chapter 3 that the introduction of these consultative rights was not a planned framework for the activities of the *Who Cares?* project. However, the re-enactment of the duty *'to ascertain the wishes and feelings'* of young people living in care or accommodation within the Children Act 1980 (Section 18 (1) was to assume major significance for NAYPIC, especially, as we shall see, in its campaigning activities.

Ban the Book campaign

Following its launch meeting, NAYPIC's campaigning activity began with the *'Ban the Book'* campaign. It was an issue that the Leeds *Ad-Lib* group had tried to do something about locally, and that young people had voiced at *Who Cares?* national meetings. But despite their determined efforts, clothing order books were still widely used in many areas. NAYPIC's campaign centred on sending a publicity pack, including an information sheet outlining their objections, and a poster, to all local authorities in England and Wales. The information sheet included:

*'Why do we object to it? Because it treats young people in care as **second class** **citizens**. It restricts our choice. We can't go to the shops we want to buy the clothes we want. Shopping for clothes is important to young people who want to look good and be able to go shopping with friends and have the same choice as them.*

*It lets the public know we are in care or somehow different. It often embarrasses young people. For example, having to wait at the check-out for a supervisor. It makes us look as though we had been shoplifting! It doesn't help young people in care to learn how to use money for themselves and be **responsible for their own lives**. A few authorities have decided to do without the order book. NAYPIC wants all authorities to abolish it.'*

However, the *'Ban the Book'* publicity, cited above, led to unforeseen consequences for NAYPIC in pursuing another key decision taken at their inaugural meeting, the decision to seek charitable status. This was essential if NAYPIC was to receive funding as an organisation in its own right. As the management committee had advocated at the launch meeting, if NAYPIC was to succeed as an organisation, it needed funding to employ staff and have its own offices. The initial application for charitable status was refused on the grounds that NAYPIC was a campaigning organisation, as the Charity Commissioner made clear to them in response to the documentation they sent, including the *'Ban the Book'* publicity.

At the time, NAYPIC was not aware of the regulations governing charitable status - if it had been, its activities could probably have been re-phrased to meet these requirements. After all 'campaigning' organisations such as Child Poverty

'NAYPIC's campaign included sending an information sheet and a poster to all local authorities'

Action Group and Shelter had acquired charitable status. In hindsight, it was partly a question of the right wording - 'educating' to increase awareness, rather than 'campaigning' to bring about change, would probably have been acceptable. But the refusal was a major set-back in that it potentially closed the door to all funding opportunities. In the aftermath, NAYPIC's management committee decided to seek legal advice on how to proceed with a future application for charitable status.

In the meantime, despite this setback, NAYPIC's work continued, sustained by the voluntary efforts, enthusiasm and commitment of its leadership and members. Its own magazine, *NAYPIC News,* was launched in the summer of 1979, spreading the word about NAYPIC including its national and local group activities, as well as providing an opportunity to recruit new members.

It was also decided to continue the *'Ban the Book'* campaign by carrying out a survey of clothing and young people in all 132 United Kingdom Social Services Departments during 1981 – the first national survey of this topic. This showed that only a quarter of responding authorities has stopped using the order book altogether. But it also provided lots of information about other aspects of clothing and young people in care, including choice and the use of money. This led to NAYPIC agreeing a clear set of policies *'to involve all young people in choices about buying clothes, and permit a sense of responsibility and dignity.'*

NAYPIC's policy on clothing

• All use of the order book should be banned, including for emergencies.

• Money should always be used. If clothing is needed at short notice an account should be held at certain shops from which clothes can be bought.

• Clothing stores should be abolished. Young people should not be made to accept second hand clothes.

• All young people over 12 should get a monthly allowance in cash for buying clothes, regardless of the kind of home they live in. Younger children should be introduced to the use of money by staff as soon as possible.

• Young people should be able to choose how money is spent, it is important for them to learn to budget. Social workers should be less protective about mistakes.

• Young people should have the choice about whether they want staff or their social workers to accompany them. They should be able to shop with friends.

- Monthly allowances should be realistic and take into account the cost of clothes at different ages and different individual needs.

- Although local areas differ in how much allowance is paid there should be at a least a national minimum. Allowances should be the same for children and young people in foster homes and children's homes.

- Children and young people in care should get separate grants for school uniforms. It is important that young people in care have a uniform if a school requires it.

'These are important changes young people wish to see as a result of their own individual experience and after considering the results of the survey.'

The findings from NAYPIC's survey gained widespread publicity including an article in the premier social services magazine, Community Care, in June 1982. The magazine featured young people holding placards stating *'Ban the Book'* and *'The Book Must Go'* on the front cover.[18] NAYPIC also gained support for their clothing policies from the Association of Directors of Social Services and professional organisations representing social workers and social care staff.

The success of the campaign, especially in regard to the publicity it received, convinced NAYPIC of the value of finding out more about local authority practices, and their impact upon young people in care. This was seen as the basis of devising its own policies and campaigns. But, first of all, it needed to find out young people's views about a far wider range of issues. This was high on the agenda of its 1981 annual general meeting, where it was agreed that local groups would be asked to talk about a range of topics in preparation for their *Life in Care* conference to be held in London at the end of 1981.

Life in Care Conference

Life in Care, organized jointly by NAYPIC and the Children's Legal Centre, was attended by over 150 young people and 50 adults from all over the country.[19] As planned at their 1981 Annual General Meeting, the young people had come prepared to talk about their experiences of care. The day was spent in small discussion groups, each group providing feedback to the whole meeting. At the final plenary session of the day it was agreed that NAYPIC should be leading national campaigns on a number of issues.

From the front cover of Community Care 3rd June 1982

Reviews and case conferences

The first of these were reviews and case conferences. These were the formal meetings that took major decisions about young people's lives, such as where they should live, how often they should see their parents, how they were getting on at school, when they should leave care and where they should live after they leave. Young people felt very strongly that they should be informed if a review or case conference about them was to be held, that they should be invited to it, and that they should also be entitled to call a case conference if something goes wrong in their lives. But for most young people who attended *Life in Care* this wasn't the practice.

One delegate, aged 17, said:

'They're planning on me going away to school and no one told me they'd had a meeting and had been saying all this stuff. That isn't right is it?'

Another young person commented:

'A child, no matter what age he is, should have the right to enter a case conference or a review. Even if you could say 'five years old - that's a bit stupid', well it can be put to him that there's going to be a discussion about him and his parents and about his background.'

Young people attending Life in Care wanted the opportunity to speak for themselves at review meetings, as well as have some say in who is invited. But they also agreed that young people should be entitled to have a friend with them at reviews if they wished.

'Young people should have some say, however small, into who attends the review so that vast crowds of people don't turn up to intimidate them.'

Running children's homes

A second topic discussed at the conference was the running of children's homes. Both staff and young people, it was felt, should be included in decisions and rule making, and they should share responsibilities for running the homes. Once made, rules should be kept consistently, not altered at every staff change, and everyone, including staff, should obey them. Nor should rules follow the individual whims of the head of home.

'There was one home where the guy was a vegetarian and no one could eat meat.'

Punishment and control

A third issue raised by young people at *Life in Care* was the use and type of punishments they were given. They felt that punishments like fining should be used for serious offences *'not silly things - like belching'*, for which three delegates had been fined! Some punishments were also condemned.

'Staff hitting young people, withholding visits and visiting parents should not be used as a punishment, some kids are more likely to rebel or crack up if they can't see their parents. Drugs should not be used to restrain kids.'

Another concern raised by young people at the event was residential staff using the existence of secure accommodation as a threat to control young people's behaviour. Also, they felt that there should be a right of appeal against being placed in secure accommodation.

Personal files and individuality

Another issue at *Life in Care* which generated a lot of heated discussion was personal files. Most young people wanted to be informed of the existence of their personal files, to be told what they were used for, and to have a right of access to them.

'If young people disagree with information on file, they should be entitled to write a note about it. All young people, whatever the circumstances, should be given their file when leaving care.'

Young people living in children's homes also felt very strongly that they were often prevented from expressing their individuality. Clothing voucher schemes, still operated by many authorities despite NAYPIC's campaign, were condemned, as was the lack of money available to give young people in care choice about haircuts, spectacles and other personal items.

Leaving care

There were also many complaints from young people about local authorities not preparing them for leaving care and not making adequate provision to support them after care. One young person suggested.

'Those under 15 should be educated towards independence by having some control over finances and sharing domestic tasks. All local authorities should make provision for young people leaving care.'

Complaints

There were also calls for young people to have a complaints procedure.

'Young people should have a complaints system in care. They should be able to go to someone, like a catering officer if they don't like the food, say you're getting eggs and chips every day. They should be able to change their social worker. And there should be an office, for example, NAYPIC, where young people could complain to.'

But as well as bringing about changes to the individual lives of young people, NAYPIC wanted to change life in care for all young people. To achieve this they believed they would have to find out more about the experiences of young people, as they had done in their survey of clothing order books. They felt that researching a topic would provide the evidence to bring about change.

Gizza Say? Reviews and young people in care

The first topic NAYPIC chose to research after Life in Care was young people's review meetings.[20] They wanted to find out what young people thought about their reviews including the extent they were involved, how they saw them, and how they could be improved. At the end of 1982 and the beginning of 1983, 465 young people living in different parts of England, Scotland and Wales, completed a questionnaire. This included 332 young people living in children's homes and 133 young people living in foster care. At that time, NAYPIC's survey was the largest that had been carried out about the views of young people living in care on any topic. And it was the first to be carried out by young people in care. Prior to the survey, those responsible for providing care didn't know what young people thought about their reviews.

Purpose of reviews

How did the young people surveyed see the purpose of their review meetings?

'Don't know, never been told.' (Young person who had spent 13 years in care).

'They talk about us.'

'Where they discover your private life.'

'You sit in the middle and they all talk about you and decide your future for you.'

'Where a social worker and some higher people talk about your future.'

'A test, an examination.'

What happens at reviews

Young people were also asked: 'what happens at your review?' Their responses to this question included:

'Usually all the people go up into a room and talk, and at the end they bring you in and tell you what's going to happen.'

'Social workers decide my future.'

'They start talking to you about yourself.'

'The social workers and teachers first go in and discuss you and then you are brought in and told of the decisions they have made.'

'At my review people put their heads together and think what to do with me.'

'They discuss what is best for me but I do not hear what they say because I am not allowed in.'

It was clear from the great majority of replies that reviews were seen as something that happened to young people, usually events being initiated by '*Them discussing,*' '*Them saying,*' '*Them deciding*'. It was seen as a powerful meeting at which young people saw their future being decided but did not see themselves as part of, even when they were present or '*in the middle*'. This feeling of impotence was described articulately by one young person.

'I feel the whole review system for me is a total facade. Although decisions taken at the review are carried out, those decisions occur through the wishes of the adults involved, whereas I am merely a bystander being informed of the decisions, not involved in its coming about.'

Cartoons by: John Kemp

NAYPIC: Head Office: Salem House, 28a, Manor Row, Bradford BD1 4QU. Tel: (0274) 728484
London Office: 20, Compton Terrace, London N1 2UN. Tel: 01-359 6251

'Decisions occur through the wishes of adults...I am merely a bystander'
The Back Cover of Gizza Say, Reviews and Young People in Care,1983

NAYPIC's survey found that a small number of young people thought their reviews were a positive experience, an occasion at which they felt fully involved.

'To see where you are going.'

'A meeting all about yourself and problems.'

'Discussing problems and talking about them openly.'

'The person has a chance to give his say.'

'It often helps clear the air on certain problems'.

Helpful reviews to young people meant openness, discussion, an exchange of views, a looking back as well as forwards, and, for some young people, a plan to assist them with specific problems.

Participation and attendance at reviews

The survey also explored young people's participation and attendance at reviews. Most of the young people living in children's homes and foster care said that they thought they should be invited to their review and two thirds replied that they should be allowed to stay in their review all the way through. But the survey found that a third of young people from the children's homes group, and a quarter of the foster care group, had not attended a review - although the vast majority of young people from both groups said they were informed when reviews were going to take place.

Many young people thought there were too many people invited to their review meeting:

'Not so many people should listen into your life.'

'I think there should be less people because if there are too many people you can get very tongue-tied and can't speak so no one hears your views.'

'Reviews I feel are too impersonal and usually embarrass me. But I feel if they could be made more comfortable I wouldn't clam up and get nervous and frightened.'

'It is not very fair to be discussed amongst a bunch of strangers.'

NAYPIC's survey found that young people living in children's homes and foster care wanted their social workers, carers, their own family and teachers to attend. As regards the presence of teachers at reviews, just over two thirds of young people in residential care agreed with them being there, but a majority of young people in foster care disagreed. There were some strong views expressed about teachers being present at reviews. As one young person put it:

'Teachers are there to teach you not to butt into your private affairs.'

Most of the young people living in a children's home or foster care wanted their reviews to be held, *'where I live'*. Only a very small number of young people in both groups thought that reviews should be held in social services offices. Their replies made this clear.

'I feel more relaxed, more at ease, free to talk.'

'I feel safer.'

'I can think clearly and relax.'

'I speak out more freely.'

'You don't feel right in somewhere you don't know.'

'You feel out of place in a strange place.'

The majority of young people surveyed by NAYPIC said that a review should last between one and two hours and the most popular time of day for reviews was the afternoon followed closely by the morning. However, not everybody was keen to have time off school, as attending reviews during school hours may present its own problems. Young people who were working were keen to have their reviews held after work, on a day off, or in the evenings or weekends.

'I think reviews should be held in non school hours because if you have a review in school time and return after the review the other children and teachers ask where you have been and if you say you've attended a review they will either 'take the micky' or will ask you what a review is, and you have to tell them it is for a children's home and I don't like people knowing I am in care.'

Reports for reviews

Two questions in the NAYPIC survey focussed upon the written reports prepared by staff about young people for their reviews. Less than a third of the young people in foster or residential care had seen the written reports for reviews and less than a quarter of the whole group had a chance to write a report themselves, although over two thirds of the young people would have liked the opportunity to prepare their own reports.

'Who are they to write things about you when they don't even know you, how do they know what really happens? Even the social workers don't know you well, apart from seeing you once every month or so. They don't spend every minute of the day with you.'

'We should be allowed to write our own reviews, if not then we should be shown what is written about us so that we can comment upon what they have written about us.'

'We never know what is going on or being said about us until we find it out. And yet so quietly, behind your back, decisions are being made about your life.'

Carrying out review decisions and making complaints

Only a small minority of young people surveyed felt that they were involved in decision making at their reviews. Most of the young people wanted a complaints system for young people in care to take their disagreements further and also make complaints when social services didn't carry out decisions made at reviews. Some of the young people living in children's homes replied that they had regular young people's meetings at which everything was discussed and they found these very helpful particularly in taking up complaints:

'We have kids' meetings so we can moan if we don't agree with anything.'

A criticism made by many young people was that review decisions were not carried out.

'I feel strongly that there should be a complaints system for young people because half of the things said at a review aren't carried out, they are either forgotten or not carried beyond the social worker.'

'Yes I do agree (with a complaints system) especially when they make promises then just don't do anything only forget.'

'I think that there should be a box so that you don't have to speak in front of people.'

Finally, a small number of young people were worried about the impact of a complaints system upon 'trust' and other dimensions of their caring relationship with residential staff.

Gizza Say? Policy implications

In the publication, *Gizza Say?* Reviews and Young People in Care, NAYPIC discussed the policy implications of its findings. It first of all highlighted the statutory responsibility of local authorities to review children and young people in their care every six months, as well as their duty under Section 18 of the Child Care Act 1980:

'...to ascertain as far as practicable the wishes and feelings of the child and give due consideration to them, having regard to his age and understanding.'

It concluded:

'It is clear from our research that there is no national policy or practice about allowing young people to attend their reviews. Some go in for the whole review, some attend for part of the review, some go in to be told the decisions at the end and some young people are never invited to attend at all. Many young people choose not to attend their review or find it a very difficult experience. After decisions have been made at reviews there is no way of disagreeing with them or in certain instances, knowing if they will be carried out. At the present time how young people experience reviews is therefore very much a lottery. NAYPIC is campaigning to improve this situation.'

Secondly, *Gizza Say?* detailed NAYPIC's policies.

• Young people of any age have a right to know what is happening to them and every effort should be made to involve them in the decisions made about them.

• Every person over 13 should have a right to attend their own reviews and to be present throughout the entire proceedings if they wish.

• Each local authority should draw up a policy about reviews which makes sure that young people fully understand the review process. This should include commitment to use language everyone can understand.

- A young person has a right to be consulted about who attends their review and their wishes to be made known to those attending the review.

- A young person should be able to choose someone they trust to help them put their point of view and back them up. This person might be a member of staff but could also be an independent outsider.

- If a young person disagrees with what is said in a review their views should be recorded along with other people's views.

- There should be a complaints system for young people to take their disagreements further and also make complaints when social services don't carry out decisions made at reviews.

Finally, *Gizza Say* identified *'issues and questions which members and local groups will be discussing during the next year and arriving at policy decisions'*.

- The position of very young children and reviews. Should they attend with a 'friend' from being very young at least for part of a review so that they gain experience and confidence?

- Should young people see reports for reviews and have an opportunity to write their own reports?

- Should young people be consulted when and where reviews take place?

- How can reviews be made a more 'comfortable' experience at which young people can openly discuss and exchange views so that they are not overawed?

- How, when and by whom should review decisions be communicated?

- Who should attend reviews? Why should they attend? These questions should pay special regard to the young person's wishes, his or her confidentiality about being in care, the position of parents and foster parents and the role of the school.

- What form should a complaints system take? What issues will it deal with and how will it work? What forms will help or hinder caring and trusting relationships?

NAYPIC, getting going

NAYPIC had got off to a good start. During these early years it maintained a high level of publicity for issues concerning young people in care in both the social work press and the national media. Its Ban the Book campaign had shown the importance of finding out what local authorities were doing, publicising their findings, and gaining the support of organisations representing managers, social workers and residential staff. Their Life in Care conference was widely reported in the press, including the Guardian, the Sunday Telegraph, Social Work Today and Community Care. NAYPIC also participated in a number of radio and television programmes including its own Open Door programme broadcast in February 1982. The findings from its first major survey in 1983 of young people's thoughts about their reviews, *Gizza Say?*, were also widely circulated.

To encourage the setting up of more local in care groups, NAYPIC published and widely distributed an action pack[21] containing ideas, hints and suggestions for young people and social workers. NAYPIC News, its national magazine, was still going strong. But its early campaigns, and, in particular, its Life in Care conference was also to provide the groundwork and impetus for what was to prove highly significant to NAYPIC's future - an opportunity to get its messages across to government itself.

Chapter 6

Sharing care

'The main argument which runs all through our Sharing Care report is that young people should have a greater responsibility in the decisions relating to their lives......more of a say in the day-to-day decision making in homes, for their rights to be made clearer to them.'

(From, Sharing Care, NAYPIC'S 1983 evidence to the House of Commons Social Services Committee on Children in Care)

NAYPIC gives evidence to the House of Commons

In July 1982, the House of Commons Social Services Committee Inquiry into Children in Care began, *'intending to look widely at a range of issues concerning the way children came into care and the way they were looked after in care.'* It made specific reference to the *'continuing and growing debate about the rights of children and the rights of parents,'* and the *'marked swing towards fostering and away from residential care'* as *'particularly pressing reasons to undertake a Select Committee Inquiry.'*[22]

NAYPIC was invited to give both written and oral evidence to the Select Committee. In 1983, it submitted Sharing Care as its written evidence.[23] This was in part derived from the work done by young people for their *'Life in Care'* conference report. But *Sharing Care* was much more than that. Whereas *Life in Care* had captured young people's views, the process of preparing written evidence provided an opportunity for NAYPIC both to set the issues in context and agree policies on key areas that affected the day-to-day lives of young people in care.

In the introduction to Sharing Care, NAYPIC advocated for three changes. First, that young people should participate far more in decision making. They cited the legal duty of local authorities to *'ascertain the wishes and feelings'* of young people, as laid down by the Child Care Act 1980, and they commented:

'Our lives are often controlled entirely by the decisions made by social workers and they are generally in a worse position to determine the best for young people in care than the young people themselves.'

Second, NAYPIC argued for more community based child care in *'small local children's homes or foster care...away from the old isolated institutions.'* They suggested that the failure to involve young people, and their separation and isolation from their local community, often resulted in practices that contributed to the stigma they experienced, as well as them being treated as victims or offenders.

Third, they argued for more consistent policies:

'The type and levels of care can vary dramatically within homes, between homes, and between local authorities, and this can increase the isolation felt by young people. We believe that a full range of community based care should be provided to all young people.'

Sharing Care provided NAYPIC's evidence of *'the major issues facing young people once they are in care.'* In doing so, their evidence tells us about what care was like for many young people during the early 1980's. To do justice to their views, their evidence is cited, as fully as possible below, with only a short introduction to each section and minor editing.

Rules, punishment and discipline

To begin with, NAYPIC, like *Ad Lib* and *Who Cares?* in the mid 1970's, highlighted the cruelty of the methods used to punish and discipline some young people, as well as the great variation in the rules and procedures experienced by young people.

'Staff that hit young people should be dismissed from their jobs, rather than just warned as is usually the case.'

'Some kids who wet the bed are made to sleep in it all night, then next night they make them sleep on the floor without any blankets.'

'It's definitely wrong to stop you from seeing your parents, it does go on quite a bit.'

'Punishment and discipline is a very important issue for young people in care. It is where young people's opinions are often most at odds with the adults who care for them. Incidents requiring discipline often happen between just two people, and then it is the adult who is most likely to be listened to. Many institutions have rules and regimes which are very strict and frustrating for the young people who have little or no say in making the rules. They can find themselves branded as 'troublemakers' or 'disturbed' just because they did not agree with the rules imposed upon them. Young people often feel that some staff can get a kick out of putting young people down.'

'Local authorities have very varied rules and procedures about discipline and punishment in their areas. Some have bothered to look at their procedures and have banned corporal punishment and other extremes in their homes, but other areas still leave a lot to the discretion of staff. Young people believe that institutions need guidelines which make sure that rules are geared towards education and learning. Institutions should be run for the young people in them, not for the convenience of the staff, and young people should have a say in how the home is run and what form of rules and punishments are allowed.

To improve the lives of young people living in care, NAYPIC made six main policy recommendations:

NAYPIC policy

1. Corporal punishment should not be administered to young people in care under any circumstances.

2. The use of physical restraint and drugs to control violent behaviour should be very carefully controlled.

3. Home visits and pocket money are a right of young people in care and denial of these should not be used as part of a system of punishment.

4. Wherever possible house meetings should be held to decide a system of rules and punishments for the establishment.

5. All young people should have the rules explained carefully to them.

6. A punishment book should be kept and be open to anyone.

Forms of control

Also in their evidence, NAYPIC raised the related issue of how young people often experienced their 'care' as 'control'. Their experiences included: being sent to 'lock ups'; punitive restrictions on their freedoms; the excessive use of restraint - violence against them, the use of drugs, and being 'thrown out' of homes to cope on their own. In their evidence they argued that young people should be given the opportunity to learn 'their responsibilities and self control' through greater involvement in the 'rules, the running of their home, and in their own lives'.

'Being put away affects kids in two ways. Either they want revenge and commit more serious crimes, or they get depressed and suicidal.'

'People going into lock-ups should be allowed to appeal to some kind of court and have legal advice and support when appealing.'

'I have never broken the law, but I was living with girls from prison who were disturbed and often violent. The place was surrounded by high walls and was patrolled by dogs. The superintendent in charge was a really sadistic man and he tried to convince me I was mad. He used to make us get up in the night and scrub floors, and he used to beat us up. Once, he twisted a girl's arm behind her back and threw her into the bath. There was no point in hitting back because he used to be a psychiatric nurse and knew all the holds.'

For many young people in care, child care is seen merely as control and punishment as the method of achieving control. This is done by the restriction of freedom and often by resorting to depriving young people of their basic needs and rights. Control becomes an instrument exercised when social workers feel that they have to enforce their authority. There are incidents when this has been taken to such extremes that violence has been used by staff on young people. This is of the greatest concern to us. But we do not underestimate the more subtle uses of control, using restraint and deprivation that occur far too regularly, by staff on young people.

The most damaging forms of control on young people are:

* *The use of drugs - the 'liquid cosh'. We also mention this under punishment, because drugs which are not used for medical reasons we regard as punishment, physically, psychologically and emotionally, and their use in this way should be banned.*

- *Being transferred to other more isolating and 'disciplinary' homes, such as Community Homes with Education (the old approved schools) and secure accommodation. Why should young people in care be locked up, when those not in care can only be locked up if they commit a serious criminal offence, or are so mentally ill they have to be 'sectioned' for compulsory medical treatment? Generally we think that transfer of young people to other placements is a way of letting residential staff and social workers duck out of their responsibilities, and not tackle the reasons as to why young people are misbehaving.*

- *We also know of cases where young people are simply thrown out of homes to fend for themselves for periods of time. This is obviously an unacceptable form of control. If parents did this they would get into trouble with social services and the courts.*

Care and control are often conceived as the same by social workers who believe that the administration of enforced control is essential to their job, many use it to make their job easier. We in NAYPIC believe that young people should learn their responsibilities and self control by having a greater involvement in the rules and running of their home and in their own lives. The co-operation and support of residential social workers is indispensable to this aim.

NAYPIC policy

1. 'Control' should be on the basis of mutual co-operation and respect between residential workers and young people.

2. The use or threatened use of drugs, transfer and suspension should be banned.

Privacy and personal freedom

NAYPIC also raised major concerns in their evidence about the lack of respect afforded to the privacy and personal freedoms of young people in care. As their views, outlined below, powerfully convey, this could impact upon many aspects of their lives, from the most intimate, to opportunities to be like other young people, in what they say, what they wear, and what they aspire to. The breadth of their concerns is reflected in their policy recommendations.

'The staff in some homes take it for granted that privacy only applies to them. What they don't realise is we are all human beings and are entitled to our own privacy however small it may or may not be.'

'There is the question of locks on the bathrooms and toilets. In some children's homes the locks are hanging off and the staff just barge in and put you in an awkward position. Proper locks on the doors would help a great deal.'

'Another thing is doors. The staff should really knock before entering and give you time to answer 'yes' or 'no'. This should be done, because in most homes the young people living there have to knock before going in to the staff rooms. A lot of the staff just treat the kids like animals and not like human beings.'

Many institutions have very little space for personal privacy. It is not expected by staff that young people need somewhere to be alone, or to have their own room. Young people in care are very restricted in how they can express their views and in many cases they cannot do this at all. For example, the head of home can threaten you with secure units if you disagree with his way of running things. Many institutions have too many locks upon doors, so restricting your movements, others have no locks on bathroom and toilet doors. In one place the girls had to bathe in their swimming costumes. In another home, teenagers had to shower in front of staff. Many young people have to dress and undress for bed in front of staff.

We feel children and young people should be afforded the opportunity for privacy both personally and with regard to their possessions. For example, children in shared rooms should at least have lockable cupboards. Local authorities should seek to ensure that children are provided with a comfortable domestic environment and that residential social workers take an active part in home making. Staff must learn that young people have a viewpoint of their own to express, and it would be better if they could encourage this rather than treat young people as if being in care meant that there was something wrong with them.

Many young people are restricted in what clothes they can wear because of an inadequate system for purchasing clothes. If you want to follow a certain fashion then it should not be discouraged. Likewise, if they wish to pursue some personal hobby or interest we feel that this should be developed and the resources provided. Many homes have too many young people in them. This can prevent some teenagers from studying, as they cannot be afforded adequate privacy, nor can they work with the noise of other youngsters, who may have little or nothing to do.

NAYPIC policy

1. Everybody, despite their race, sex or outside appearance, should be treated equally.

2. 'Problem youngsters' or those whose personal history dictates, need the same respect as those who have not had this labelling. There should be no distinctions between deprived and depraved.

3. The right to information, with the support of a social worker, on who we are and what can happen to us.

4. The need for a personal record, memorabilia and belongings.

5. The right of privacy and the respect which that accords.

6. The right of freedom of expression, and for any criticisms or suggestions to be taken constructively.

7. Confidences of a personal nature should be confined to whoever it was told to.

8. The right to be involved in any decisions that are made about our lives.

Reviews and case conferences

As discussed in chapter 5, the first topic NAYPIC researched was young people's thoughts about their reviews. This resulted in their '*Gizza Say*' publication, based on the views of 465 young people. This included NAYPIC's policy on reviews which was submitted as evidence to the Inquiry, along with the comments outlined below. Both '*Gizza Say*' and NAYPIC's evidence highlight the wide variation in practice between local authorities as regards attendance at reviews by young people, who else is invited to their reviews, and the lack of an appeal system.

'All young people should be told if there is a review or case conference about them, and should be invited to it. They should also be entitled to call a case conference if something goes wrong.'

'If a decision was made that a young person did not agree with, we thought that they should be able to appeal against this decision, and if necessary have the review re-done.'

'Who should be invited to your review? The people in charge of you and the people who know what you are like, and I think parents should also go to the review.'

'I would like to go to my own review to see what they said, and maybe tell them how I feel about what they said.'

By law all young people in care are supposed to have their situation looked at every six months. This is called a review and it can happen in a variety of different ways. If everything is going well and everyone appears to be happy then the social worker may just discuss the situation with his or her boss. If there are problems or there is likely to be some change in the young person's life, then the review can involve many more people. This is sometimes known as a case conference.

At the present time there are no rules about who should be at a review except the young person's social worker and a senior member of the social services department. But it often appears to young people that the more problems there are the more strange people turn up at a review. Young people seldom have any say in who attends their review and they are often surprised and upset when they see how many apparent strangers will hear about the often painful and difficult details of their lives. They often have strong feelings about the people who attend, e.g. they do not always see why school teachers should attend if the issues are not directly concerned with school work or attendance. They would also like to be asked about their parents' attendance.

There is no national policy about allowing young people to attend their reviews – some young people do attend and some don't. Some go in for the full session, others go in to be told the decisions at the end. Often young people choose not to attend their review because they feel outnumbered, they do not know the other people and do not believe that what they have to say will really be listened to. After decisions have been made at reviews young people have no way of disagreeing with decisions that are made.

Files and records

At the '*Life in Care*' conference, 'personal files' was a hot topic. Important questions for young people included: could they see their files, who else has access to their files, and was the information contained within them accurate? In *Sharing Care*, NAYPIC raised young people's concerns and made policy recommendations to bring about changes.

'Young people should have the right to see their files and they should be told that there's a file on them. If there is anything that a young person disagrees with, they should be able to place a notice on the file that this wasn't how they saw it.'

'Young people should have their files actually given to them when they're 18 or when they leave care.'

'In care there are a lot of truths that you don't get to know about because you are too young or not able to understand, or just are simply not told about.'

All young people in care will have files kept about them containing details of their family life before coming into care. These will include reports from doctors, psychiatrists and social workers on the young person's progress and behaviour whilst in care. Young people do not have the right to read their own files though some do with the permission of their social worker and others find out by 'borrowing' the key to the filing cabinet.

Many young people feel that too many other people are able to read their files even if they cannot. They believe that much of what is kept in these files can be very much one person's opinion of what is happening. The file does not usually include their views. Particular events can be seen as important years after they have happened and if they are left on file young people in care often feel unfairly weighed down by past reputations. Even people with criminal records have a chance by law to start again, so why can't they? They believe that there should be a regular 'spring-cleaning' system for records of children in care.

NAYPIC policy

1. All young people should have the right to read information kept on them. If that information is painful they should be given support to cope with it.

2. Young people should have a right to add their own comments and opinions to the file.

3. More control should be kept of who has the chance to read young people's files.

4. Local authorities should set up a system to 'spring-clean' files at regular intervals, preferably in consultation with the young person concerned.

5. The system of keeping information and the reasons for doing so should be explained to any young person coming into care.

Foster placements

NAYPIC was concerned that the drive to increase fostering placements, although welcome for some young people, should not be seen as the only, or best option, for all children and young people. In *Sharing Care* they drew attention to poor foster placements. Their main concerns also informed their policy recommendations, including the importance of foster care training, having ongoing contact with social workers, and, critically, being more involved in the process, from advertising to choice of foster placement.

'I have been fostered for 17 years. My foster parents treat me like their own daughter, they treat me the same as the rest of the family.'

'In some of our meetings we have talked about fostering. Most of us in the group have been fostered in the past, although now we all live in children's homes. Although fostering sometimes works it is not always the answer. Some of us feel that we were treated differently from the foster parents own children and we were given fewer privileges.'

Fostering has become the main trend in social work today. It is seen as the main alternative to residential child care. The growth of fostering is starting to change the use and structure of social services resources. It is seen as the fashionable answer for the many children and young people who have previously been termed 'hard to place.' NAYPIC is in no way opposed to fostering, on the contrary we support any increase in the available opportunities, as part of the consumer's choice. However, the development of fostering cannot be done at the expense of good community care through the break up of the residential or nursery care sector.

Recent lessons in the horrors of fostering failures are only part of the picture. The work done by one social work department, in Scotland, shows a staggering amount of breakdowns in fostering within the first few months. The effects of this kind of activity on the young person involved have not been taken into consideration. What is disturbing is that fostering might be considered as the norm and that anyone who cannot fit into this, or who doesn't want to, may suffer because of the pressure put on them.

The lack of support by social services after care is also an alarming factor in a fostering situation. Our experience shows that many young people are unaware of the position they will be in, and once in that position they have no right to return to their previous foster home.

NAYPIC policy

1. Fostering should be encouraged as an option. Young people in care should be able to be fostered if the circumstances are right.

2. Local authorities should not put young people with foster parents, simply because it is cheaper than keeping them in a residential home or school.

3. Not all young people when trying to find foster parents will want to be advertised in shop windows, local papers and magazines. Local authorities should always consult young people before placing any advertisement, if the child is old enough to understand. Young people who do wish to be advertised should be encouraged to write their own piece for advertising.

4. More training of potential foster parents about care and children and young people is needed.

5. Once fostered contact between the young person and social worker remains very important. Young people should be told where they can contact their social worker.

6. Young people should be allowed to leave their foster parents if they so wish

7. Young people should have some say in who they want to be fostered with. To do this, they should be able to visit a few possible foster parents before being offered a short or long term placement.

Education and care

In their evidence, NAYPIC also identified many of the problems young people experienced at school, including the stigma arising from lack of confidentiality surrounding being in care, the lack of support and encouragement for their learning, and the bureaucratic hurdles for those going onto further and higher education. In their recommendations they wanted the 'encouragement, support and help in care' to overcome difficulties, as they would get from 'a good parent'.

'Sometimes they bring your personal life up in front of other kids. I don't like this because it embarrasses me and I don't want everybody to know that I'm in care.'

'If you're in care the teachers know much more about your private life and background than they know about other kids.'

'Recently a teacher said to me in front of everybody 'I hear you're doing much better in a home'. This made me feel like walking out.'

We feel that the many problems that attach themselves to young people in care whilst at school could be reduced if young people's right to privacy, as well as continued support and help for them, were guaranteed. There can often be terrible stigma suffered by young people if the details of their home life are known. 'Why can't we just be treated like everyone else' is a familiar plea made about school life. It is often not by choice that a young person's teacher is made aware of the problems that a young person may have had to contend with. Young people would prefer to choose the people that are given information about them and to decide how much information they should have.

Some young people feel that teachers have no place in case conferences and reviews, whilst others appreciate the input of a teacher – as someone whom they might trust. The choice of who should be involved should really rest with the young person themselves. There is nothing to stop a head of home from enquiring, just as other parents do, about the progress of their 'charge' at open days.

For those young people that do get a place in some form of further education there may be worse penalties. NAYPIC finds it unacceptable that Social Service Departments often neglect their duties in providing an adequate grant. Too often, the Social Services Department and the Local Education Authority may play-off against each other, hoping that they do not have to accept responsibility for the young person. If the spirit of the law were followed then Social Services would, like good parents, accept that they should maintain and support a young person through a period of further education, even after they have left care.

NAYPIC policy

1. Young people should have every encouragement, support and help in care, especially those with difficulties in learning, as they would get from 'good parents'.

2. All attempts should be made to decrease the institutional stigmas attached to young people in care whilst at school.

3. Teachers should not have access to information that young people themselves are unaware of. Young people should have a right to control how much information about themselves teachers have and who it is passed on to.

4. Social Services should accept that they have the responsibility, regardless of age or status, of maintaining and supporting young people through further education.

Clothing order books and allowances

As discussed in chapter 4, NAYPIC's *Ban the Book* campaign had publicised its opposition to clothing order books – an issue first raised by the Leeds *Ad Lib* group in 1973, ten years earlier. NAYPIC's campaign agreed a clear set of policies which were included in Sharing Care. In addition it noted:

The use of the clothing order book, or voucher system, for purchasing clothing for young people in care has been widely condemned by local authority associations, the Association of Directors of Social Services, the British Association of Social Workers, the Residential Care Association and others, but yet this system is still used by many local authorities. Many departments have changed their practice in recent years and abolished or restricted the use of the order book. However, a number of authorities continue to use it and some, confusingly, have come out against the order book at a policy level, but still allow their homes to use it in practice.

Race and care

Before the 1980's very little attention had been paid in research, policy and practice to the experiences of young people being 'black and in care'. One young person had written about the 'governor' of a children's home being 'colour prejudice' in *Who Cares News* in 1979. But it was at the *Life in Care* conference in 1981 and the subsequent preparation of their evidence, *Sharing Care*, that NAYPIC brought the issue to the fore. This also laid the foundations of the creation of the *Black and In Care* group, as described in chapter 7.

'Being black and brought up in a white middle class foster home and then leaving to discover I don't fit into black or white society, is a real kick in the teeth.'

'Being in care is bad enough, but being black and in care is twice as bad.'

'I was told not to play with black boys because they would get me in trouble.'

Discrimination on the grounds of race or sex is against the law. It has also become more widely appreciated in society that the differences in people's cultural backgrounds should be respected. It should be recognised that they need support and encouragement so that they might build their confidence in themselves.

Young people of a minority race or culture can have a difficult time in care. Generally they are expected to adjust their way of thinking to the white, male, middle class or Christian view. The reality of their background or surrounding environment can be in direct conflict with this. Foster homes can also be a problem. Young people may need to have a greater understanding of their cultural history and information on rights should be provided. Also, where education occurs within the institution, it should include study on culture.

Cultural and racial differences should be recognised and where there are different values and beliefs these should not be looked upon as the young person having an 'identity problem', or being 'disturbed'. We feel that there is a need for more awareness about the development and behaviour of young people who may identify with their own ethnic group and who may require knowledge about that culture.

Again, we stress that if homes were to run open meetings of their own then an atmosphere of equality and democracy might help in advancing young people's confidence and understanding in themselves and each other.

NAYPIC policy

1. More social workers in both field and residential work should be recruited, from different ethnic origins.

2. A young person's religious and cultural background should be maintained if he or she wishes, and should not be discouraged.

3. Where racial prejudice or discriminating behaviour is proved to cause harm or hurtful feelings, the persons involved should be severely disciplined or dismissed.

4. All guides for young people entering care should include a section for young people from ethnic minority groups outlining their rights and freedoms. They should be able to seek and have access to further advice if necessary from their local community relations council.

Sex and sexuality

Issues related to sexual behaviour and sexuality whilst young people were living in care were another neglected area. In their evidence, NAYPIC drew attention to a range of issues including: a culture of silence surrounding sexual development; the reinforcement of traditional gender stereotypes in day-to-day domestic roles, and in staff attitudes to sexual behaviour; a failure to respond to the needs of pregnant young women and young mothers; and a lack of recognition of the potential sexual abuse by staff and having polices in place to deal with it.

Sex and sexuality is a problem in both single and mixed institutions. Very little is done to help you cope with your sexuality and your identification with those of the same or different sex. What is required is an atmosphere of understanding by the staff and more education on the general issues of sex.

In so many institutions there exists a tense atmosphere surrounding sex and your feelings about it. There is no encouragement to be open about how you feel about your sexual development. This, of course, has implications for you when you grow up, resulting in further problems in adulthood relationships. Some single sex institutions can force unwelcome sexual contact with staff and young people. Roles of the different sexes too can be strongly divided in many homes. For example, male staff and boys are not expected to do the washing up.

Many places will refuse to take in teenage girls because they are seen as a problem. Teenage girls, like boys, will be engaging in sexual activities but the consequences for girls, if it becomes known to staff, is different: often labelling them as being promiscuous, and they could be moved to another place, whereas boys will not suffer any degrading looks, resentment, or be sent away. Girls who get pregnant are more often than not told to leave the home and are placed in inferior accommodation for mothers and babies.

Sanitary protection is a highly personal area for girls but staff often pay little notice to a girl's need for privacy. Bulk buying gives them no choice of different models or brands. Girls are checked up on whether they are having a period or not to see if they are pregnant. This means they have to show their sanitary towels. Often, male staff are sent with girls to shops when buying these items.

Information on what young people can do about sexual advances and abuse by staff and by other young people should be made available. These young people should also be made to feel that they will be safe if they want to inform the authority about sexual abuse.

NAYPIC policy

1. All staff should be trained in how to deal with sexual problems.

2. All young people should be able to express their feelings about sex without fear of recrimination from staff. Young people should not be regarded as deviants or given special treatment for their behaviour.

3. Contraception should be made available to those of age regardless of the viewpoints of staff.

4. Decent and non-segregated facilities should be available to girls in care with babies.

5. Girls should not be excluded from the democratic process in a home just because they are female.

Young disabled people in care

In their evidence, NAYPIC also highlighted some of the issues facing young disabled people.

We feel that the social services do not do enough to help disabled young people to become independent or help them to have their own homes and to run them. Many young people end up in long stay hospitals, old people's homes, and other unsuitable institutions. Often the good work done for them when they are under 18 can be completely destroyed when they reach adulthood. The lack of interest and resources means that rather than independence they can only look forward to a life of further dependence. Provision needs to be made available for disabled young people of all ages. However, they should never be excluded from the normal daily life of a home nor be treated any differently because of their handicap.

NAYPIC policy

Disabled young people in care should have the right to:

1. As normal a life as possible, including integration into ordinary homes – both foster homes and community homes.

2. Opportunities in housing, leisure, education and employment to fulfil their individual potential and lessen the effect of their disabilities.

3. Opportunities for choice and participation in decision making.

4. None of these rights should be limited by financial consideration.

Complaints

At the time NAYPIC submitted its evidence, very few local authorities had formal complaints procedures for young people living in care, or ways of resolving problems when difficulties first arose between young people and staff. In *Sharing Care*, NAYPIC proposed a fully independent complaints system, as well the need for regular house meetings in children's homes to deal with 'both complaints and suggestions'.

'She was very strict. She used to hit us for talking in bed, though it was hard to fall asleep those summer evenings because the curtains were thin and we went to bed very early. Sometimes, if she caught us chatting she would make us stand with bare feet on the stone floor in the washroom and lock us up in the dark, which really frightened me. But who could I turn to?'

'The point is, young people who want to make a complaint have to get there first before the staff get on the blower and put their end first.'

'I don't know who to complain to, to get the problem solved.'

Very few local authorities have a complaints procedure. Some that do publicise the fact and the procedure in guides or booklets, but these are very few indeed. We welcome the individual effort of these authorities and feel that it should be adopted by all the other local authorities. It is important that an address be available in a booklet so that young people know that they can complain to their social services department rather than their home or field worker. This would be preferred by

'A complaints system should be available to every young person in care'

many because complaints given to social workers can get lost and recriminatory action could also follow by residential staff, without the knowledge of the social services department.

A complaints system should be generally available for every young person in care to have a fair hearing in any serious disciplinary situation. This should involve an outside independent person and the young person should have some support in putting their views across. However, a complaints procedure would be more effective if it could be open to any young person who feels that they have a grievance or who wants to report some action or activity which they feel to be wrong, concerning their life in local authority care. There is an urgent need for an official complaints procedure known to every young person in care and it should involve a panel of people not employed or involved with the social services.

NAYPIC would support any proposals for a new and independent complaints procedure to be set up. However, this cannot be done in isolation. All through this report we have stressed the need for young people to be more involved in the running of their home and we feel that a complaints procedure should fit into an overall commitment to allowing young people to voice their feelings and opinions and for them to see that suggestions and complaints will be acted on.

A formal complaints system would not then be the only form of action for redress. And many smaller cases or incidents would not have to go through a lengthy and perhaps complicated procedure. If a complaints system is the only outlet it would also become a very busy one. The best way of dealing with both complaints and suggestions is for this to be taken up within house meetings with the knowledge that a higher authority exists, should this be inadequate.

Leaving care

The problems and challenges faced by young people leaving care to live independently was initially highlighted by the Leeds *Ad-Lib* group in 1973, and subsequently by *Who Cares?* in 1977, and by NAYPIC at their *Life in Care* conference in 1981. *Sharing Care* provided NAYPIC with an opportunity to bring together the accumulated knowledge from these different strands.

Leaving care, particularly for those who came into care at a young age and who have lived in care ever since, can create very mixed feelings. Many young people do look forward to 'getting out' of care and being in control of their own lives, but often shortly before they leave they start to become frightened and worried at the prospect. Most young people will be totally unprepared to manage on their own, especially after having everything done for them whilst in care. Many young people are expected to leave their homes at 18. We feel it is totally unrealistic for the social services to care for someone one day and then to expect them to fend for themselves the next.

Many local authorities are failing in their duty as good parents to young people in their care. We can estimate that thousands of young people leave care totally unprepared after spending years in local authority children's homes and hostels, because they have reached the age of 18. Authorities are not under any duty towards them once they reach that age and they may be left to find accommodation for themselves in depressing bed-sits or unsuitable hostels.

How young people make out when they leave care is influenced by very many factors. Some of these are major social problems such as youth unemployment and the frustrations and poor income that this means for young people. However, young people leaving care may be more disadvantaged than others in relation to job opportunities. Local authorities cannot be expected to provide jobs for young people leaving care but they can help. There are three broad areas where young people could be helped to overcome the considerable problems they face when local authorities finally turn their backs on them. These are: preparation for leaving care; accommodation; support and financial assistance after leaving care.

Preparation for leaving care

Even though there has been a strong trend away from large institutions, many community homes nowadays can involve 12-20 children and the cooking and cleaning is on a larger scale than the average family. Food, cleaning materials, toilet rolls and the like are bought in bulk and domestic or care staff plan and cook meals. Some authorities have also introduced planned menus and pre-cooked frozen foods. It is often considered impracticable for young people coming up to 16 or 18 to begin to use local shops to buy individual portions of food and then to cook these in the home. With no idea of the cost of living and domestic and personal budgeting, young people often get into severe difficulty within the first years of leaving care: add to that the isolation and intolerance suffered and you can see that the provision of housing alone is inadequate. Rent, rates, gas and electricity bills or meters, the cost of food and clothing can all be a nightmare to someone who has only had limited pocket money to spend in the past and who was relatively free of the worry of the essentials of life, all of which were provided by the local authority.

We know of young people who have spent their whole wage or giro on the first day; of others not knowing how to use a gas meter or not realising that electricity bills come in quarterly and have to be saved for. All these things need to be discussed before the young person leaves care, not thrust upon them a week or so beforehand, if at all. This advice should also be supplemented by the guidance or experience of others who have left care, you shouldn't feel that you are stepping out into unknown territory

To have seen other young people leave and disappear without trace means you have no visible contact with the possible traumas of the outside world. It would be beneficial to those who are still in care as well as those who have left, if residential homes could keep their doors open and encourage ex-care people to return. The pressure to become independent keeps young people from returning as this can be seen as a sign of not being able to cope. Transferring young people to a foster home during their final period in care should not be viewed as a means of providing support for young people. They can also lose their foster home at 18 and may indeed end up more disadvantaged than if they had stayed in a community home.

Accommodation

'He is now 23 and has never had a place he could call home. He was taken into care at the age of two and lived in various children's homes until he was 16. After leaving care he was initially fixed up with digs in a house of a Catholic family in South Leeds, but he wanted more independence since he didn't have his own bedroom. For several years he travelled round the countryside getting seasonal employment. He squatted in a hotel and after being evicted by the police, lived for two weeks leading up to Christmas in a tent on a building site. He is now sleeping on the floor of a friend's flat, since the council had turned down his application for housing.'

The usual facility open to young people leaving care is some form of 'halfway' accommodation, like boys' or girls' hostels. In some areas there has been a move towards providing lodging schemes (with selected landlords and landladies), and cluster flats or group housing schemes where one selected person may benefit from free accommodation in return for making himself available to give support if needed to other tenants who will all be within one or two years of leaving care.

Some exciting new ground has been opened up in providing flatlets within some community homes which, depending on their size, can be used by one or more of the older residents as their own base where they live virtually independently. The importance of these few available resources is that they allow young people the support of being part of a community, should they require it. However, other resources for young people leaving care are virtually non-existent. Young people need some choice in deciding where they would like to have their first independent home on leaving care. It is a sad fact of life that many young people are put into bed and breakfast accommodation, others rely on friends and some are forced into squats, or living rough. Social services departments need to have a better relationship with the housing department.

We feel that it is a scandal that a charity for homeless people like Shelter should have had to become so involved in the issue of young people leaving care because local authorities are unwilling or unable to recognise where their own responsibilities lie.

Support and financial assistance

Whatever resources are made available, and we feel that young people leaving care should have as wide a choice as possible, it is not enough merely to get someone placed in some accommodation and expect them to get on with it. Life can be very different and difficult when you are on your own, when previous links have been cut there is a need for continued help and support. When young people first leave care they do need fairly major financial help, for example in furnishing a bed-sit, buying linen, pots and pans, crockery and cutlery and clothes to wear for work and college or job interviews. Every local authority needs a clear duty to provide financial assistance. The present law under Section 27 of the Children's Act 1980 is not sufficient in reminding local authorities of their real obligations. It seems like a concession for young people rather than a right. The law allows policies and practices to vary wildly, consequently many young people leaving care can get a very raw deal indeed.

As a group NAYPIC is greatly concerned about the awful things that can happen to young people once they are out of care. We feel that with continued support and use of resources many of these problems would hardly exist. At the moment the prevailing notion in some authorities seems to be that young people leaving care will either 'sink or swim'- if they sink then they may be forced to rely on other social services and thus use up valuable resources. Lack of support can mean that young people get led into a life of destitution, drug abuse and prostitution. As a group NAYPIC is greatly concerned about this. We feel that with continued support many of the problems faced by young people leaving care would be lessened, that they would not be forced into relying on resources from other social services and that they might quickly become really independent and self-reliant.

What is needed is greater preparation whilst in care, resources made available when you are leaving and the continued help and support of someone who you know will be around and whom you can trust. The whole area of preparation needs to be given more emphasis in social work training and in service training. They could invite members of a local NAYPIC group along to speak to social workers or social work students about the general problems which they face in care and their views on how they can be tackled more effectively. This could also be extended into the area of accommodation: in Bradford ex-care members of NAYPIC are involved in a housing venture which allows young people leaving care both the provision of a flat and the necessary support to go with it.

Ideas which arise include a 'crash pad' or weekend facility for those who find themselves in particular difficulties after leaving care. Advice on welfare rights, and on careers training and further education opportunities can also be crucial. Young people in care often have their education potential underestimated and it may be only after having left care that opportunities to fulfil a hidden potential can be explored and pursued.

NAYPIC policy

1. Every local authority should have a policy which lays guidelines about how a young person should be prepared for leaving care and make sure establishments are organised to allow this.

2. All young people should have experience of doing their own washing, budgeting and cooking.

3. There should be more half-way establishments which allow greater freedom but with some support.

4. Every local authority should provide some support and advice service for young people out of care as they learn to cope alone. This would include temporary accommodation, weekend stays, information and advice on education, welfare rights, accommodation, etc.

5. Every local authority should have a budget which would allow each young person leaving care to have a realistic grant towards setting up on their own, e.g., furniture and household goods.

6. Social workers should receive more adequate training in the issues which face young people leaving care.

Finally

In concluding their evidence NAYPIC highlighted the key principles underpinning their specific policy recommendations: increasing the involvement of young people in decisions which shape their lives; having a range of community based care, including foster care and children's homes; and support for extending the role of NAYPIC to contribute to improvements in policy and practice.

The main argument which runs all through our Sharing Care report is that young people should have a greater responsibility in the decisions relating to their lives. We feel that this extends into and beyond the particular type of care they have and are under. We would like young people to have more of a say in the day-to-day decision-making in homes, for their rights to be made clearer to them, and for a satisfactory structure to be provided so that the process can start operating effectively and efficiently. We feel that the government can help in its child care legislation by making the involvement of young people possible by law and by making existing law both clearer in its intention and wider in its application.

NAYPIC would like to add that in its view the move towards community based care is good social work policy and should be continued and extended. This means a wide availability of care within the community - we do not see fostering as an inevitable progression of this - it should be seen as part of the overall picture. It should not be seen as an obvious alternative nor as succeeding residential care, or as being somehow more 'natural'. This view is damaging both in implication and practice.

The cutting back of residential care is of the greatest concern to us. Community homes are a valuable asset which should not be closed. The face of social work is pock-marked with the faults and failures of past fashions and trends. We need to keep options open for the future.

We would like more support from local authorities and residential workers so that NAYPIC groups might be encouraged to develop. This would give young people the chance to have an independent liaison group with social services. This is most important as many social services are now looking at some of the ideas for change that we've mentioned in our report.

Any child care policy changes which are made must involve those who will be affected by them. Young people in care will only accept social services policies for care if departments accept young people as those with the real knowledge of what being in care is about. Six years ago Who Cares? put together for the first time a Charter of Rights and a list of Things We Want to Change (discussed in chapter 3). Six years later these have not yet been fulfilled.

Sharing Care and the state of care

Sharing Care showed, from a young person's perspective, the very poor state of state care at the beginning of the 1980's. In their evidence, the young people's voices echoed many of the concerns raised during the previous decade, initially by the Leeds *Ad-Lib* group and later by *Who Cares?* The state didn't care enough about its most vulnerable children and young people to ensure that they were all provided with the quality of care to help them overcome the problems they had come into care with, and to maximise their opportunities in life. As a consequence, many were condemned to a life of control, misery or indifference, including for some young people, further abuse by their 'carers'. In that sense their 'care' still owed more to the legacy of the poor law than the new professional social work thinking. And it was left to young people in care, themselves, through their own organisation, NAYPIC, in their evidence to the House of Commons Social Services Committee to show how their future might be made better than their past.

Sharing Care and NAYPIC's future

NAYPIC's momentum during its early days came mainly from the enthusiasm and commitment of a small number of young people who gave their time freely. They gained 'on the job' experience in running a national organisation, including its administration, finance and publicity. The priority afforded to the work and activities of local in care groups meant that this experience was not just restricted to those young people on NAYPIC's management committee. National campaigns were also local campaigns. The *Ban the Book* campaign had been particularly successful in involving local groups and several social service departments acknowledged that they abolished the clothing order book in response to the activity of local groups. The *Life in Care* conference had also involved local groups. Their preparation for that event provided the foundation for Sharing Care, NAYPIC's written evidence to the House of Commons Social Services Committee on Children in Care cited in this chapter. This was to prove highly influential, not only in respect of its impact upon the committee's recommendations and the government's response (as was to become clear later when both these reports were published), but also in relation to their funding application. *Sharing Care* convinced senior civil servants and ministers that NAYPIC should be supported.

Remarkably, what NAYPIC had achieved to date, was by the voluntary efforts of young people, a small and very able group who led the work nationally, supported by a small group of committed adults. But if they were going to continue to develop as an effective national organisation they needed funding, and since their application for charitable status had been turned down they had received none. The legal advice they received, following their earlier rejection by the Charity Commissioners, was for NAYPIC to set up a separate organisation, the In Care Company, as a charitable wing, to pursue charitable status.

As this was being progressed, NAYPIC were advised that they could apply to Government for funding. They also decided, in view of their earlier rejection, to send the In Care Company's application for Charitable Status in draft form for comment by the Commissioners – to test the waters before submitting their formal application. The funding application to Government was sent off on 4th December 1982 making it clear that the In Care Company was being set up to progress their requirement that NAYPIC obtain charitable status. However, on the 30 December 1982, the Charity Commissioners wrote to NAYPIC informing them that the draft documentation they received from them would not be acceptable.

'It seemed to us then (referring to NAYPIC's initial 1979 application) as now (referring to the current, 1982, In Care Company's application) that it was a group mainly interested in campaigning for administrative change.'[24]

In August 1983 NAYPIC heard that they were successful in their grant application for 3 year Government funding. But their failure to secure charitable status did pose another dilemma for them: without it they were unable to receive and administer Government funding as an organisation in their own right. In the event, and with agreement of all stakeholders, the National Council of Voluntary Organisations (NCVO) agreed to administer the Government grant. The Government also made it a condition of acceptance of the grant that an Adult Advisory Group to NAYPIC be set up.

August 1983 marked a new phase in NAYPIC's development. For the first time in its short history it had received funding for its activities from the Government. This enabled NAYPIC to employ two full time workers, both who had been in care themselves, and have its own offices. One worker was to be based in London at the offices of the Children's Legal Centre. The second worker was to be based in a new office, to be opened in Bradford. It meant that NAYPIC would have a 'North' and 'South' presence and could begin 'full time' work.

Having heard NAYPIC's oral evidence and having received *Sharing Care*, the House of Commons Committee, in its 1984 Report on Children in Care commented, '*NAYPIC's growth has given children a voice of their own.*' [25] But looking back to the circumstances surrounding the ending of the *Who Cares?* project in November 1978, it might have been a very different story. NAYPIC may never have got off the ground in the first place. There is little doubt that the commitment of the members of the *Who Cares?* Action group, and the momentum they generated, was far ahead of the professionals who had planned the *Who Cares?* project. The Action Group wanted something more than just being part of a professional project, '*listening to the voices of young people.*' They wanted a national membership organisation that could bring about changes to improve the lives of young people living in care. It was the setting up of NAYPIC that marked the beginnings of the right's movement for young people in care. The story of Leeds *Ad-Lib* and of *Who Cares?* would have been of interest as innovations, creative local group and national project initiatives. But without NAYPIC their stories would have had little coherence. There would have been no rights movement. Citing NAYPIC, the House of Commons Committee on Children in Care, stated, '*children's rights are now being recognised as never before.*' [26] The next stage in NAYPIC'S journey was as a funded organisation with its own full-time staff. New work was planned including a conference on being *Black and In Care*.

Chapter 7

Black and in care

'The most valuable resource of any ethnic group is its children. Nevertheless black children are being taken from black families by the process of the law and being placed in white families. It is in essence 'internal colonialism' and a new form of the slave trade, but only black children are used.'

(The Association of Black Social Workers and Allied Professionals, Evidence to House of Commons Select Committee, 1983, Children in Care[27])

Being black and in care – the context

During the early 1980's two separate surveys, carried out in London and Manchester, showed for the first time that children and young people from Afro-Caribbean backgrounds were significantly over-represented in care, and the *'children of mixed parentage alarmingly so'*.[28] In the context of heated debates surrounding racism in society at that time, and what was seen as the failure of 'cultural pluralism' or 'cultural diversity' approaches in progressing greater equality, the position of black children in care was to echo wider concerns.

During 1983, this was reflected in evidence submitted to the House of Commons, Social Services Committee Report on Children in Care. The Association of Black Social Workers and Allied Professions (ABSWAP), cited above, viewed the practice of trans-racial placements as *'a microcosm of the oppression of black people in this society'* and saw the failure to collect official data on ethnicity as a *'conspiracy of silence'*.[29] The Commission for Racial Equality (CRE) in their evidence to the Committee suggested that:

'Black families have imposed on them eurocentric assumptions of good parenting and proper family life which are used to justify separating parents from children.'[30]

The CRE also highlighted the failure of social service departments to recruit enough black foster and adoptive parents, resulting in black children being over-represented in children's homes. They also expressed concerns that when black children were fostered with white families this could lead to 'identity problems', including a poor self-image, lack of cultural knowledge, few black friends and a stereotyped white view of young black people. In their evidence to the House of Commons Committee, the London Boroughs Association (LBA) commented on the failure of social work to engage with black families in rehabilitating children:

'Child care officers were known in the West Indian community as 'Farewell Workers,' as once they became involved in a family it was 'farewell' to the children.'[31]

Planning the 'Black and In Care' conference

Some of these issues, especially those relating to the experiences of black young people living in children's homes, had come to light during NAYPIC's *Life in Care* conference and in the subsequent preparation of *Sharing Care*, submitted as evidence to the House of Commons Committee on Children in Care in 1983. During 1984, the Children's Legal Centre employed a black member of staff to collaborate with NAYPIC in setting up a national conference to find out more about the experiences of black young people living in children's homes and foster care. A Black and In Care Steering Group (BIC) was set up in 1984, and weekly meetings took place to plan the event, to decide where the conference should be held, who should be invited and the issues to be discussed.[32]

'One of the things that the Steering Group felt strongly about from the beginning was that our conference was for young black people in care and ex-care, and some black social workers, and not for young white people or white social workers. This was decided because we felt that black people would feel inhibited from expressing their views fully in front of white people and especially white social workers.'

'We got a lot of stick from the press about this issue - we were called black racists, black activist guerrillas and Trotskyites. We got several complaints from white social workers about the fact that they were to be excluded from the conference.'

We had to explain to them that this decision had been made by young black people in care and ex-care themselves, many of whom had suffered because of the racist attitudes of white social workers.'

A member of the BIC steering group wrote about why she became involved:

'I got involved in the Steering Group organising the conference because I have only become aware of my colour in the last couple of years. Growing up as a 'white person', I went through an identity crisis and then I met young black people who first plaited and combed my hair. When I left care, I ended up in the black community and at first felt afraid of black people. Black people couldn't realise why I didn't know of black food and culture such as history and reggae music and West Indian dialects. Now I have learnt about black culture and I am aware of racism within the child care system - including the way they took me out of the black community and put me into the white community so that I lost my identity and could not find out about my culture.'

Black and In Care conference

The first Black and In Care conference in the UK was held at Kingsway Princeton College, London on Saturday 20 October 1984. About 300 people attended the conference which included 180 young black people in care or ex-care, and 120 black social workers and community workers. The young people came from London, Liverpool, Derby, Sheffield, Birmingham, Manchester, Devon and Bradford.

The day included contributions from members of the steering group and feedback from five young people's workshops. The workshop topics had been identified by the steering group as the most important issues affecting young black people in care in their everyday lives: culture, health, hair and skin care; mixed parentage; racism in the care system; fostering and leaving care. Each of the groups was asked to make recommendations for policy and practice. A *Black and In Care* conference report was prepared and published in May 1985.[33] As well as reporting on the conference this also included poems, drawings and prose.

The main contents of the report, capturing the feedback and recommendations from the workshops, are outlined below with only minor editing.

Front cover, Black and In Care conference report, 1985

Culture, health, hair and skin care

'We had heard a lot of young black people in care complaining that they were not getting the right type of skin and hair creams (if any) whilst in care. Other people complained that our hair was often cut very short as soon as they got into care because the white workers did not know how to handle it. There were others who said that they were not given any information about sickle cell anaemia and other aspects of health that have particular relevance to black people. So this is why this topic was chosen.'

This workshop had a wide variety of participants who were of all ages and from many different parts of England.

'All children are treated the same in care. That is, we all have the white image projected on us. This means that if you are black or non-white you don't really fit in. The children in care are brought up in an environment in which black food is alien. They are thought of as abnormal if they ask for hair oil etc, because white children don't have the same type of hair as the majority of black people. The social workers and foster parents didn't seem to understand that the majority of black kids suffer from dry skin and therefore need a good moisturising cream.'

Recommendations

1. The black child needs to be put in an area where there are some black people or other black families, who they can identify with.

2. Black workers should be encouraged to be employed in social services and in homes, because they give the kids a much needed link with their culture.

3. Black children from the same family should be kept together.

4. The staff should be educated about sickle cell anaemia, and they should try to ensure that all the black kids are screened for it to ensure that they can be treated appropriately.

5. The child should be encouraged to find out things about his/her culture and the staff should be able to show them the positive sides of their culture.

6. The children should be encouraged to eat all different types of food from different cultures - a menu with West Indian or Asian food appearing at least once within the week.

7. The staff should be educated in how to look after hair and skin of children from different cultures to ensure that the correct hair and skin creams are given.

8. Foster parents should be examined to ensure that they are aware of these issues and are doing something positive about them.

Mixed parentage

'It was obvious to us that in proportion to the population, there were too many young black people in care (in the inner city areas sometimes up to 60 per cent). But out of this number a large percentage are of mixed parentage. These children were often called offensive names like 'half-caste' and 'half-breed' as well, therefore this topic was chosen to discuss the specific difficulties of such children and young people.'

Twelve young people attended the mixed parentage group. All were of mixed parentage except one young man. The workshop began with the offensive names they were called.

'Half-caste', 'coloured' and 'olive skinned', for example, are words which should not be used. First, because the words came from white people, and the first word stems back from slavery meaning half white which is offensive. Second, white people are not pure white but they are not labelled. If social services are talking of a mixed parentage person they should say 'mixed parentage' or 'black'.'

It was recognised in the group that knowing you are black can be positive. But if you are mixed parentage then you cannot push aside the white side of yourself. Also, it was felt that your definition of yourself should go beyond your colour. In the workshop it was agreed that the teaching and learning has to come from the residential social workers, whether they are black or white, as well as the individual.

'If you have knowledge of your culture maybe you would not accept labelling such as 'half-caste'. The young people themselves should define their colour, not others above them.'

In the workshop discussion it emerged that some staff treated lighter-skinned young people better than the darker-skinned young people. Also, one young Asian woman said that she was brought up as a white person, but social services placed her with an Asian foster family. This placement broke down because she did not know of her culture. It was agreed in the group that the person being fostered should have a choice of black, white or 'mixed-race' foster parents.

Recommendations

1. If you are of mixed parentage you should be called mixed parentage.

2. Young people being fostered should have a choice whether they want to be fostered with white, black or 'mixed race' foster parents.

Racism in the care system

'This workshop was vital because of the racism which exists in society as a whole which is reflected in the care system. Although racism would be mentioned in other workshops, it was felt necessary to have a separate workshop to discuss how it affected young people in care and also suggestions for change.'

The poet Lemm Sissay, who had been in care himself, contributed a poem to the event, published in the *Black and in Care* Conference Report (1985).

Black Rap

B.L.A.C.K.
Where do we stand in the world today?
get back! to the back of the queue
black and who are you?
black spot, black mark, black stain, black pain, black! B.L.A.C.K.
where do we stand in the world of today?
get tripped, fall on your face
nigger boy ain't gonna run in my race
keep him on the floor an' kick him more and more keep him on the floor an'
kick him till him sore
black black he's nigger and he's black
kick him in the head and kick him in the back black! B.L.AC.K.

where do we stand in the world of today?
well I've got no time for subtlety
to give you what you want from me
I've tried and tried an' all have lied
I've tried again and again 'an again but all my tryin' has been in vain an' now
I'm left cryin' on the floor left in rags an' I'm so poor under these rags
which I wear is me! yes I'm their nigger boy nigger boy yes I'm their nigger
girl nigger girl
black!!
B.L.A.C.K.
where do we stand in the world of today?
now that they know I'm black they ask me where I live oh why do I feel that it's
all take and no give
I say Mister Officer I'm in a children's home
they say hey step back you're on your own.

Almost everyone in the group had experienced racism of some kind. Some young people had been called a 'black bastard', while others had more subtle remarks at meal times or when programmes on Africa were on television. Also, it was felt that help and advice on culture was denied to young people and this made many reject their culture when leaving care and going into the black community.

In this group many young people said that they were taken out of the black community from the start of their time in care. They were sent to 'white places' - often in rural areas, small towns or suburbia. This made black young people feel that they were being deliberately taken from their community. Even the staff who should be educated to work with young black people often knew very little about black culture. One young person had to go to his local library to learn what little he could from books. When another young person tried to talk to a member of staff about his culture he was told '*you don't have to worry about that you're in England now, you know, when in Rome*'.

When racist comments were made to them, young people felt useless, especially when senior staff did not take their complaints seriously. It was agreed that a system should be designed for young people to make complaints and offending staff should be disciplined. It was felt that if staff really cared for young people they would try to encourage them to learn about their culture. They would also understand how being brought up in white middle class areas isolated black young people from their own communities.

Recommendations

1. Disciplinary action must be taken on those staff who make racist remarks or comments to young people.

2. References to young people's cultural backgrounds and history should be made available to young people in care.

3. Funds should be made available for young people to visit the countries of their origins.

4. Black people should be encouraged to work in the social services as residential and field social workers.

5. Families must be kept together and should not be split up when going into care.

6. The young people should not be 'shipped out' of the black community into rural areas where there is no black community.

Fostering

'Up until recently, most young black people have been fostered by white middle-class people and this has resulted in many of us having 'identity problems'. We thought it was important to have a workshop on the whole question of fostering, including discussion on trans-racial placements and 'hard to place' teenagers.'

The fostering workshop discussed whether it should be compulsory that black children and young people be fostered with black parents, or whether it should be the young person's choice. But what if a young person chose a white foster family because they had been brought up in a predominantly white environment? Two young people in the group said that they were confused when asked about whether they would like to go to black or white foster parents. They had been brought up in a white environment in Liverpool and had no real black identities. The young people were aware of the difficulties of living with foster parents, even if they were black foster parents, especially if they were fostered in their teens after living in institutions run mainly by white staff.

'We feel it is important that young black people should be aware of their culture and be prepared for the racism they are going to face in the community they may live in.'

The way forward

Black Children Need Black Families

Could you foster a child?

The way forward — a black social worker's view.

The day conference on October 20 1984 on 'Black and In Care' was an historic occasion and marks the beginning of what one hopes will be a new era for black people manifesting the ability to assert their rights and themselves. The irony of this event was that it took place in the year when some white politicians felt that they should take an anti-racist stance by declaring 1984 Anti-Racist Year (there were several rallies and meetings organised by the Greater London Council).

Black people in general, including black children and young people in care, know that one year is not going to make that much difference unless there is a clear commitment to constructive change for our benefit. As far as black children and young people in care are concerned, the Black and In Care Conference was in my view the beginning of positive moves for improvement of conditions and a deepening awareness of the issues involved.

Those of us who shared the experiences of the conference are now posing the question: what now? Bearing in mind the fact that 1985 is International Youth Year, this question is most appropriate. Perhaps the answer is a simple one. There will be more, lots more. But that is too easy an answer for anyone to give. We all know, for example, that adults are very good at making promises but not that good at delivering the goods.

So before answers are attempted, the Steering Group may wish to assess and take into account the effect of the experiences on their personal growth. Once completed, they may wish to consider in real terms the overall impact of the event. Having satisfied themselves, they may then wish to consider the necessity to capitalise on the momentum of that day in October and set about to:

1 encourage local authorities to find black families for black children in care, especially offering local authorities adopting this policy guidance and advice at a price;
2 establish with NAYPIC a set of guidelines re: good care practice with a black perspective for all those involved with institutional care;
3 seek sponsors from the black business community/local authorities to run seminars on skin and hair care and health;
4 engage in educational workshops;

40   41

'Up until recently, most young black people have been fostered by white middle-class people and this has resulted in many of us having 'identity problems'.
From the Black and In Care conference report, 1984

A member of Black and In Care wrote:

'I was brought up in Essex and the town I lived in did not have any black community or even many black families. I have not yet read my file but I was told that there were no black foster families in the area to foster me. I was, however, fostered three times and they all broke down within a few months. I do not remember being unhappy about the families that I was placed in but now I wish that I had been in a black family. I feel that it would have made my life in the last few years easier. I felt a stranger in the black community and felt that I didn't belong there. I can also say that if I had been asked between the ages of 13-17 years old whether I would have liked to go into a black foster home I would have said 'no'. This was because I did not identify with black people, as I had not lived or hardly ever seen any black people in the areas I lived in. I never had a black social worker in all my time in care.'

Recommendations

1. Young black people should have the choice whether they are to be fostered with black or white foster parents.

2. Black adults should be involved in the fostering and adoption process involving a black child.

3. White people fostering young people should be educated about black culture.

Leaving care

'We chose this topic because many young black people do not have the opportunity to get to know the black community after having been isolated from it for so many years.' A member of the steering group captured her experience of leaving care in the poem, 'It's bad for your child to be in care', cited below:

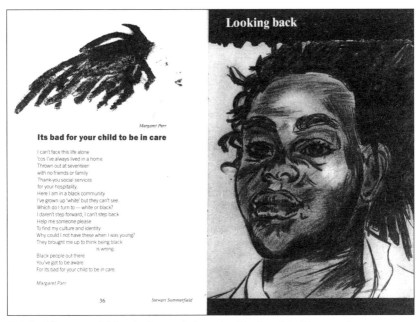

'It's bad for your child to be in care', from the Black and In Care conference report

Before discussing 'leaving care', the workshop had a general discussion of what it was like being brought up in a children's home. The group highlighted that there are predominantly white staff in children's homes. Because of this, black children in homes get used to 'white life' and accept it - they don't know any better. Some young black people had to push for things like Afro-combs which should be in all children's homes where black children are resident.

It was recommended that white staff should go on racism-awareness courses. It was also recommended that when the *Black and In Care* group is organised it should visit children's homes to educate other young black people about their lives including their culture, roots, healthcare and cooking. It was felt that there should be more 'black activities' in children's homes to help young black people relate to black people, such as books, posters and outings to black galleries.

The group also agreed that young black people in children's homes should have the option to cook their own meals, if they did not like English food. They should be encouraged to cook black foods by black and white staff. Some young people commented that there was friction between black young people and some white staff who did not like reggae music. It was felt that the social services 'management' should include some black bosses, not just white senior staff.

Another recommendation was that there should be weekly courses for young black people, for example, in a youth club where there would be a programme of 'black activities'. It was also felt very strongly that young people in care should keep in contact with their families and that social workers should encourage this. Where there were no black staff in the home, young black people in care were often completely ignorant about factors concerning health relating to black people, including sickle cell anaemia. There was also the problem that many young people in care lived in far out places where there were few black people which made them feel isolated, especially when there was no chance of getting any 'black' entertainment.

On the question of leaving care, it was thought that it would be a good idea to have courses specifically preparing young people for leaving care, to help them learn how to cook food, wash, clean, and generally look after themselves. The prospect of leaving care was often frightening for many young people, both black and white, because they get used to their surroundings at the children's home and they are scared of being lonely when they leave. For young black people it was especially important that they should have the opportunity to get to know the black community before leaving their children's home.

The provision for young people leaving care was felt to be inadequate. The accommodation arranged for people was often of a poor standard. Young people found it difficult to pay bills, rent and manage money on leaving care, and felt they should have the opportunity to learn how to budget whilst in care. Members of the group thought that a big problem was that when you are in a children's home you often have everything done for you, and when you leave you don't know how to do things for yourself.

NAYPIC and Black and In Care

The Black and In Care Steering Group and NAYPIC had succeeded in bringing young black people in care and ex-care together with black social workers to discuss their experiences of care. The initial controversy surrounding a conference just for black young people and black workers generated a lot of interest. This led to members of the BIC group carrying out interviews for radio, television, and magazines, as well as reaching professional audiences at conferences and training events.

The *Black and In Care conference report* published in May 1985 with the set of recommendations (cited within this chapter) was widely circulated to local authorities. This revealed a 'white care' that failed to recognise many of the needs of young people who were 'black and in care' at that time. This included the neglect of culture and identity; ignorance about diet, health, hair and skin care; the lack of black and minority ethnic foster carers and staff in children's homes; racism within care; a failure to recognise the identity issues for young people of mixed parentage, and the separation from family and community and the problems this created for young people leaving care.

As regards the future, the group also received funding to make their own video.

'To express it you have to feel it, and when you feel it you will never forget it. And that is what we have done on video. We express our experiences and feelings of what life is like when you're black and in care. We talk about the problems we face and how we overcome them or are still trying to overcome them.'

The Black and In Care steering group continued to meet for a year after the conference to *'carry on our fight to help black young people in care and ex-care'*. But they worked closely with NAYPIC, at a national level and through membership of local NAYPIC groups. In terms of the future, NAYPIC was seen by Black and In Care as the organisation to bring about change for all young people in care, including black young people.

Chapter 8

'Wishes and feelings'

'The growth in the status of the National Association of Children in Care representing the 'pure consumer interest in child care' is a welcome opportunity for children to make their views known.'

(House of Commons, Second Report from the Social Services Committee, Children in Care, 1984)

'When I left care I felt that I had been pushed out with no help whatsoever... I would like to see my file... At this home they have to buy everything in bulk, they send us order forms from County Hall so there is no choice, we all have to use the same toothpaste and soap. Tampons and towels are purchased the same way... It is a scandal that order books are still used by some young people for buying clothes.'

(Views of young people from NAYPIC's surveys, discussed below, carried out between 1984-1988)

Listening to young people

During the 1980's the views of young people in care were much sought after and this was reflected in policy and practice as well as research studies carried out during these years.[34] As detailed in chapter 6, NAYPIC submitted its own evidence, *Sharing Care*, to the House of Commons Committee on Children in Care during 1983. Its unique role and future potential as an influential 'consumer' and 'rights' organisation was acknowledged in the Committee's 1984 Report to Parliament.

'Children's rights are now being recognised as never before, both in theory and practice. The growth in the status of the National Association of Young People in Care representing the 'pure consumer interest in child care' is a welcome opportunity for children to make their views known. The growing conviction that children have, or should have, enforceable rights as individuals, even within a general tradition of liberal paternalism, can be expected to have a major impact on the whole field of child care over years to come.' [35]

The Committee's report although introducing many of the 'rights' issues in respect of young people in care, held back in some of its recommendations, for example, in relation to complaints procedures. But, as will be discussed later, it did pave the way for significant changes that were to be introduced by the Children Act 1989. Also, as the report suggests, the 'recognition' of rights was sustained during this period. This was reflected in references in policy and practice documents, not only to children's rights, but also more generally to consumer involvement and participation in public services.[36]

The work of the Children's Legal Centre and their monthly bulletin *Childright* were pertinent in keeping a high profile for rights issues relating to children in care and other vulnerable groups of young people during the 1980's. They campaigned for the views of young people to be given far more prominence and for young people to have the right to independent representation. They also campaigned against what they saw as oppressive state policies and practices, including the administration of corporal punishment in children's homes, and locking up children in care.

Bringing about change for young people in care was NAYPIC's mission. They already had some success in their campaign to *'Ban the Book*,' with the result that more young people were given money to buy their clothes, instead of using order books. They had also persuaded some local authorities to *Gizza Say?* – so that more young people could attend and speak at their reviews. Both these campaigns were grounded in NAYPIC's own surveys. This was their way of finding out about young people's experiences, devising policies, gaining publicity for young people's views and using the findings to bring about change. In carrying out surveys, and using them as a way of changing practice, NAYPIC made explicit reference to Section 18 of the Child Care Act 1980, including the duty on local authorities to *'ascertain as far as is practicable the wishes and feelings of children in care in making decisions.'* NAYPIC viewed Section 18 as providing the legal framework for their activities. They believed that by surveying and presenting the collective evidence of young people's *'wishes and feelings'* local authorities would have to listen to them.

Building on the success of these earlier campaigns, NAYPIC took the decision to find out what young people in care thought about other policies and practices. Between 1984 and 1988 this included young people's case files, leaving care, guidebooks for young people and sanitary protection for young women in care. Significantly, for the first time since NAYPIC began, they employed paid staff to carry out this work.

For Whose Eyes Only? Files and Young People in Care

NAYPIC's survey of personal files set out to explore a number of questions that young people in care had raised both in their local groups and at national events. These included: are young people allowed to see their files or not? Is the information contained within their files correct? And do young people want to see their files? During 1984, to find out the answers to these questions, NAYPIC sent a postal questionnaire to young people aged 13 to 19 living in care all over the country. As expected, many local authorities refused to take part. However, from the 40 local authorities which did respond positively, a total of 455 replies were received. The report, *For Whose Eyes Only, Files and Young People in Care* was published in 1985.[37]

Seeing their file

NAYPIC's survey found that although most young people were aware of the existence of files only a very small number of young people (just 11 per cent) had actually seen their file. Some of the young people commented that they did not know they *could* see their file. The survey also found that young people did not know how many other people had seen their file, why they had seen it, and in what circumstances. Most of the young people surveyed were also unaware of the types of information kept in their files.

'I was never told files were kept on me, but everyone should know about their past.'

'My idea of a file is that people have written down everything they could find out about me, but as I have never seen it I wouldn't really know.'

'I would like to see my file to understand why a punishment has been exercised on me.'

'I would like to see my file to check up on the social workers and to find out who my real parents are.'

'I was not allowed to see any of it. It was read out to me.'

Information and accuracy of files

NAYPIC's survey also found that young people were concerned that a lot of information was based on the opinions of staff and not on what they considered as facts. As one young person commented:

'Files should not be based on opinion, only fact. Only relevant information should be included.'

Just under half of the very small number of young people who had seen their file said it contained accurate information about their lives. Nearly all the young people surveyed (97 per cent) wanted to check their files for accuracy, either with their social worker or by themselves. Many young people commented on this:

'All files are dangerous if the information is incorrect. They should be checked for validity by the person concerned.'

'I should have a right to check my file because I sometimes wonder whether people write the truth about me.'

'I would like to find out how my file has grown so big.'

NAYPIC's research showed that while most young people (just over 80 per cent) agreed that information should be kept about them, they were concerned about the amount and type of information that was collected and stored:

'I think information should be kept but only as much as is helpful, but not the personal stuff.'

'As little information should be kept as possible but as much as is needed.'

'They don't need half the information they've got especially the personal details. Some of what is written is only done because it gives them something to do.'

'A file is part of you and your life and should be private, if kept at all.'

Access to files

NAYPIC's survey showed that instances of young people being allowed to see their files were very rare indeed. Access to their personal files depended on the knowledge young people had of where their files were kept, by whom, how many files there were, and critically, who to contact to see their file. When young people were asked who they would contact if they wanted to see their file, two thirds said, '*their social worker.*' However, of the young people who had seen their file, just over three quarters had done this by contacting the residential staff at their children's home. Many young people blamed their social workers for not allowing them access to their file.

When young people were asked if they were aware of exactly who could see their file, just over half surveyed did not know, or thought that only the police could see them. A small number of young people thought that anyone who worked with them, or other workers who wanted to, could see their file. Many young people surveyed commented on the invasion of privacy:

'*I feel it is wrong that anyone can see something that is so personal. They should be kept under strict security and only authorised people should see them.*'

'*My foster parents were allowed to see my file, so why can't I?*'

'*Social workers should have the power to show you your file.*'

What happens to files when young people leave care?

The survey also found that young people were unaware of what happens to their file when they leave care. Most young people (96 per cent) surveyed said they would like to receive their file when they leave care. Young people were also asked what they would like to do with, or have done with their file, when they leave care. Just under two thirds said they would like to keep it, while just under a third said they would like to destroy it.

Policies and procedures

When reporting their findings in *For Whose Eyes Only?*, NAYPIC concluded that there was no national or local policy governing young people's access to their files, or procedures to check if the information contained within it was accurate, or to challenge, or to change any of the information. They were also concerned that young people were being denied access to their past, to their own story.

'*Young people need to understand the past in order to create a future for themselves, but despite this many young people become lost in the care of a local authority, and decisions regarding their welfare are often taken without due regard either the child's best interests or the child's wishes.'*

NAYPIC's findings showed that the practice surrounding personal files, like that relating to reviews, in their earlier *Gizza Say* survey, was a lottery. Some young people were allowed to see all their file, other young people were only allowed to see part of their file, some young people were not allowed to read their file but have it read out to them, while other young people were not allowed to see their file at all. Finally, in their report, NAYPIC identified questions to be discussed by young people in their local groups that would contribute to the formulation of NAYPIC's policy.

- Should all young people be told of the existence of files when they enter care, who can see them, and why they are needed?

- Should they have the right to see their files, check them, correct them, and wherever possible be allowed to participate in their formation?

- Should all information contained in files be based on fact, and not opinion?

- Should all information be relevant in order to provide an effective service for those in care?

- Should social workers ensure that all information is correct, up to date, factual, and relevant?

- Should social workers listen more to the needs of those they are providing a service for and help them to understand why certain actions and decisions have been taken?

- Should the carers work towards decreasing the stigma (both inside and outside care) that young people feel, access to files being only one step towards this goal?

- Should access to files whilst in care be realistic rather than tokenistic so that young people can prepare themselves effectively for life outside care?

- Should social workers have the authority to allow access to files and the information in them so that the young person does not get lost in the maze of bureaucracy, inherent in all areas of local government?

- How can third party information be protected so that the privacy of everyone is maintained?

- Should such information be checked for its validity before it appears on anyone's file?

- Should painful information be read by the person it concerns and should they be helped to cope with this?

- When files are no longer in use should they be destroyed or given to the person concerned?

- Should there be clear statements given to everyone in care explaining their rights? Above all those in care should be treated as the human being they are and accorded the same respect.

'I've Never Been So Lonely': A survey of young people leaving care

As described in chapter 2, the very first in care group in the country, Leeds *Ad Lib*, was set up in 1973 so that young people who had recently left care, and were coping with the challenges of living independently, could share their experiences with those about to leave care. The *Who Cares?* project also did much to highlight the lack of practical preparation for young people leaving care, particularly in its regional group meetings, and in its publications including *Who Cares? Young People in Care Speak Out,* Who Cares News and its Ruskin Conference Report.

NAYPIC continued to carry the leaving care torch. Since it began in 1979, it had also actively campaigned to improve conditions for young people leaving care. The problems faced by young people leaving care, were voiced at their *Life in Care* conference and included in *Sharing Care*, their evidence submitted to the House of Commons Social Services Committee on Children in Care in 1983. During 1984, NAYPIC received a grant from The Royal Jubilee Trust to help fund a survey of young people's views about leaving care.[38] Altogether 157 young people completed a questionnaire. This comprised an *in care group* of 79 young people, aged 15 to 18, who were still living in children's homes and foster care, and were due to leave within three months to three years time, and an *out of care group* of 78 young people, aged 19 to 21, who had already left care within the last three years.

In care group of young people

For the 79 young people still living in care at the time of completing the questionnaire, the main aims of the survey were to find out: their experience of preparation including practical skills and the use of money; their present placement and their choices of accommodation on leaving care; their views on the support received after leaving care; their educational and employment circumstances; and their 'main worries' about leaving care.

Practical preparation

'When I was in a children's home they never taught you the domestic side of life, how to sew, cook, clean, wash and iron or to handle money.'

NAYPIC found that nearly two-thirds of the in care group was gaining experience of cooking, washing, ironing, and cleaning but this still meant that a significant minority, about one-third, who were due to leave care within a relatively short time, still had no experience of these very important practical areas. An equally disturbing finding was that a small number of young people were still regularly using order books to buy clothes, even at 15 plus years of age! The survey found that most of the in care group had talked about leaving care with someone, the majority with their social worker or residential worker, although 14 of the young people replied that they hadn't specifically talked about leaving care with anybody. A majority of the young people thought they were being prepared to handle money.

Accommodation

'I think it is wrong that when you reach the age of 18 you have to leave where you live, kids living with their parents don't often leave home until they are in their 20's or get married.'

'When we leave care why should they stop caring?'

'Why should I leave when I come of age when I want to stay in my present accommodation?'

NAYPIC's survey showed that most of the in care group were expecting to move from their present accommodation at between 16 and 18 years of age. As the young

'A significant minority of young people who were due to leave care still had no experience of very important practical areas.'

people's comments, reveal, the expectation of leaving at that age made them feel different from other young people, specifically: '*kids living with their parents,*' another, perhaps final, example of the stigma of care which many young people feel. The survey found that those young people who were expecting to remain in care, in their present placement, were mainly living in foster care. The accommodation choices of the young people surveyed, in order of their preference were: furnished and unfurnished flats; being in their own or a shared house or maisonette; bed-sitting accommodation; and lodgings. Not surprisingly, NAYPIC's survey found that most young people were worried about accommodation.

'*I think that the waiting list for a council flat is too long and I don't want to go into a grotty little bed-sit. I think at least some council flats should be reserved for kids leaving care in each borough.*'

'*The council always want to throw people leaving care into very poor flats, and when we argue they leave us there for years and the only way out is getting pregnant.*'

The great majority of the young people wanted to stay in the area where they were currently in care. As one young person responded:

'*If I get any accommodation I would like it in the same estate that I am living in now because if I get into difficulties I could easily contact my foster parents, plus I have made friends with people on this estate.*'

Also, just under half of the group replied that they would like to share their accommodation with someone.

'*I would like to be with a friend or friends who I know.*'

Continued support and worries

NAYPIC found that most of the young people surveyed wanted to keep in touch with their social worker, residential worker or foster parents, when they left care. Very few young people said that they didn't want continued contact. Most wanted to be supported by those who had offered them help whilst they were in care, although this wasn't their expectation.

'When you have been in the same home for a couple of years you get to know all the staff and always have somebody there to talk to but when leaving care you don't have anybody.'

Nearly half the young people were worried about leaving care and their main concerns were about being alone and coping without money or practical skills.

'My main worry is getting kicked out of the front door and being left to survive on my own.'

'I worry about being alone, having nobody to talk to.'

'Will I be able to find a flat and a job, will I be able to cope on my own?'

'I worry about being on my own and having to do everything on my own, being unemployed and paying bills.'

'I am worried because I won't be living with parents, only on my own, and as I haven't got a proper job how can I support myself.'

'Being lonely at night.'

'Anything else to say'

In response to the final 'open ended' question: 'anything else to say'- one young person wrote.

'People who have been in care a long time tend to be very unconfident with people, and have no real sense of identity. They behave how they think whoever they are with would expect them to behave instead of just being themselves. It is institutions which causes this. I believe that if smaller places were available, then care wouldn't have to be as routine as it is at present, and more time and attention could be paid to those who need it. Also, less 'organised' activities could be done, which could try and force children out into the world to meet people and make friends out of care.'

After care group

For the 78 young people who had already left care during the last three years, the survey aimed to find out about: their past experience and views of preparation and budgeting; their accommodation circumstances and changes since leaving care; their experiences of support by social services, their friends and their family, including financial assistance; their employment; and their 'main problems' since leaving care.

Practical preparation

NAYPIC's survey found that the majority of the young people did have experience of cooking, ironing, washing and cleaning whilst in care but nevertheless a minority, about 20 per cent, said that they were not prepared in these important skills. More significantly, just over 40 per cent of the young people had not been given the opportunity to budget and use money whilst living in care. Also, just over a quarter of the young people replied that they didn't know how to register with a doctor or dentist when they left care. Overall, just under half of the young people said they didn't think they were well prepared for leaving care. Responses by care leavers to the question, *'What preparation would have been helpful to you?'* included:

'Teaching me self confidence, in fact I was frightened to ask for anything at all.'

'To show you how to handle money, to show you what bills mean.'

'Contraception advice, water bills etc. I don't understand how to read them although I pay them.'

'Learning how to spend money, pay rent, rates, gas and electricity.'

Accommodation

NAYPIC's survey found that most of the young people had moved at least once since leaving care and a small number had changed their accommodation frequently. Since leaving care, nearly two-thirds of the group had lived in a flat, a third of the young people had lived in a house and a quarter had lived in lodgings. For those who had moved regularly, their accommodation also included bed and breakfast accommodation, squats, sleeping on friends' floors, and hostels as well as boarding houses for homeless people. Just over half of the young people were sharing their accommodation at the time of completing the questionnaire, and over one-third said that they were dissatisfied with their current accommodation. Their complaints included:

'When I applied for a flat the people at the housing department started asking me questions: why do my parents live in another town and I live here? Why was

I put in care? I don't think my family background has anything to do with getting accommodation.'

'This one bedroom flat is not suitable for me and my baby, also it's damp.'

'This flat is too small and it's not in the area where I was brought up.'

'The condition of the flat is terrible. It is damp, faulty light switches, door handles falling off.'

'The boarding house I live in is too much like an institution.'

Continued support, financial assistance and problems

NAYPIC's survey found that on leaving care nearly 40 per cent of the young people did not receive any financial assistance from their social service department. Of those who did receive financial help there was considerable variation in the amount of grant allocated, from £30 to £300. Some young people were given small 18th birthday gifts of around £10 and from their response it was clear they assumed this was their leaving care entitlement. Other young people were given second hand bedding and furniture, and one young person had the ultimate practical preparation experience of being accompanied by a member of staff with an order book to purchase sheets, pans and cutlery! A majority of the young people surveyed were maintaining contact with their social worker or residential worker and had received help from them since leaving care. Perhaps not surprisingly most of the young people said that they found leaving care a very hard and difficult experience. The *'main problems'* identified by the young people were:

'Living alone and loneliness.'

'Being on my own, you are always with people in care but not anymore.'

'When I moved out I never felt more lonely in my life.'

'My biggest problem was being homeless, this led to crime.'

'I have just left care. I feel very lonely and sad. I am very angry about when I was in care, they never bothered to help me find any of my family or tell me properly why I was in care. I didn't know about my mother until I was fourteen and that was because I took my file and read about her.'

'When I left I just felt as though I had been pushed out with no help whatsoever.'

'Being lonely' was often reinforced by unemployment and the subsistence level 'dole' that young people were trying to exist on. Advice from the 'out of care' young people to help other young people still in care included:

'I know from my experience it's not as great as you think. Don't rush into it. Find out about benefits, housing, find out everything you can.'

'Teach them how to cope with so called freedom.'

'When leaving care, keep in touch with staff and friends. Don't cut yourself off or you will feel lonely and depressed.'

'Yes I left care and went to London to live. I was utterly alone. When I left my hotel job, and therefore my living space, I had to squat. I had a really hard time and were it not for the fact that I was into clubbing it I might have easily become a prostitute. Any road I took might have been a degenerate one. Fortunately I got married and have stayed relatively OK since. But young people just out of care need other people.'

'Just providing young people with money and a place to live is not enough. Social services should provide parental support until your mid twenties if you want it.'

'I think when you first leave care you ought to share with a friend, because I found the first month awful. I kept going back to the home and crying.'

'At first when I moved into my flat I didn't go out much, and once I was poorly and I was depressed. I could have been dead and no-one would have known or been bothered.'

'I think there should be an allowance for all children leaving care to help alleviate the burden and financial strain of setting up home.'

One young person wrote at length about her experiences in response to NAYPIC's survey.

'When I left care I thought all my problems were over. It couldn't have been further from the truth. At the age of 16 I left care and moved into a flat, just after leaving school. I had all the pressures the same as any adult at such a young age. I didn't get an allowance for bedding or anything else and found it very difficult

coping with buying furniture and other things. It meant I had to work evenings as well as days to buy essential items. As everyone knows, a 16 year old does not earn as much as an older experienced worker, so I had to work twice as long hours to cover expenses. I also found it hard to live by myself. Being brought up in care, living with many people in a household without ever being by yourself, it was very difficult to live on my own and learn to like my own company.

Lack of parental guidance, changing situations so quickly and living with such responsibilities at such a young age, and not being able to develop any personality gradually, like most teenagers in a normal upbringing, makes you very unstable and very vulnerable to deterministic pressures. I think there should be after-care counselling to help with such mental pressures. After all, teenagers brought up by parents who leave home, leave by choice, whereas a child in care does not have this choice, and not having a choice is a pressure in itself.'

Policy implications

In discussing the policy implications of its findings from both the 'in care' and 'out of care' groups, NAYPIC noted:

'Most of the issues raised by the findings of our survey are not new ones. It is therefore depressing that still so many young people are inadequately prepared in terms of practical skills and handling money. It is also surely a scandal that order books are still used by some people for buying clothes and that leaving care grants continue to be such a lottery. The case for all young people wherever they are in care receiving a grant at a defined level seems overwhelming.'

In relation to accommodation policy, NAYPIC questioned the logicality of young people being 'evicted' from care at 16 to 18 years of age:

'This seriously questions the commitment to 'in loco parentis' responsibility, particularly if the parental model to be adopted is one relative to the transitional period for most young people not in care, who usually remain at home until their early twenties (according to Social Trends 1984).'

NAYPIC also highlighted their finding that most of the young people had found themselves alone at some time and that *'being lonely'* was perhaps the biggest problem, made worse by unemployment:

'More thought needs to be given to neighbourhood, friendship and family links whilst young people are still in care, so that sustained supportive relationships are 'carried over'.

Guidebooks and young people in care

It was the experience of NAYPIC members, in the handful of local authorities which provided them, that guidebooks about life in care were highly valued by young people living in both foster homes and residential care. Their members had found them very helpful in a number of different ways: first, in answering many of the questions raised by young people about living away from home for the first time, in what seemed to many of them as a very complicated and bureaucratic system of legal requirements and local authority practices; second, they helped explain to young people their rights and responsibilities, as well as the expectations of their carers and families; third, the information contained within the guide gave young people an opportunity to raise issues with their carers and social workers, including an avenue to complain about their care; finally, it was the experience of NAYPIC members that guidebooks encouraged openness and young people's participation whilst living in care.

In order to find out what was happening in different local authorities and actively encourage social services to provide guidebooks for young people in care, NAYPIC carried out an 'action project' between 1984 and 1986.[39] This included: a survey of all social services and social work departments in England and Wales, Scotland and Northern Ireland; sending these departments examples of 'good guides' which were currently in use; meeting with interested departments to discuss how a guide should be prepared, who should be involved, and what should be included; and providing interested departments with NAYPIC's own *'Recommendations for Guidebooks for Young People in Care'*.

NAYPIC's survey showed that only 22 per cent of the large number of authorities surveyed (92 per cent of all authorities in the UK) had prepared guidebooks for young people in their care by the end of 1986 - even though it was as long ago as 1979 that the first guidebook had been produced by an English local authority. The survey found that by the end of 1986 there was not a single guidebook in existence in Scotland, and only a small number (14 per cent) of the large rural county councils had provided them. It also showed that just over a third of the London Boroughs and a fifth of the urban Metropolitan Districts, had introduced guidebooks.

In Northern Ireland, the boards responsible for children's services were instructed to prepare guidebooks following the abuse revelations in the Kincora Boys Home. They dutifully did so but with little consultation and involvement of young people, residential workers and other interested parties. As a consequence, the guides were conceived very narrowly, primarily as a complaints procedure for young people in residential care. By the end of NAYPIC's survey in 1986, 45 per cent of the authorities surveyed had no plans to introduce guidebooks for young people in care.

The 'action' part of the project was based upon NAYPIC members' wide experience or reviewing existing guidebooks, as well as assisting local authorities with the preparation of guidebooks. This resulted in the following *Recommendations for Guidebooks for Young People in Care*, sent to all local authorities:

Preparation and participation

'It is very important that the guidebook is drawn up by a working party with representatives of young people in foster and residential care, foster parents, residential workers, fieldworkers and management. It may also be useful to consult with local groups or organisations such as NAYPIC, and professional associations representing staff. Once a draft copy has been produced it would be helpful if it was sent to NAYPIC for comment.'

Presentation and distribution

'The front cover should be appealing and colourful, encouraging young people to read it. Cartoons and pictures should be used wherever possible to illustrate points. Jargon words and phrases used frequently in laws, should be explained clearly in the guidebook. All sections of the guidebook should be clear, concise and descriptive. There should be an easy index enabling young people to locate specific sections. Young people find alphabetical order the easiest and most helpful. The guidebook should be personally addressed to each individual young person.'

Content

'The guidebook should contain a short introduction from the Director of Social Services. Topics in the guidebook should cover important issues to young people in care. The guidebook should take into account the differences in race, gender, religion and disabilities of the young people. The guidebooks should list and

define the different 'sections' (legally) of care. The guidebook should have a space where the young person's social worker/key worker could explain why the young person came into care.'

'The guidebook should aim to include typical questions that young people ask whilst in care and after care, with direct answers.'

'The guidebook should contain a list of useful organisations with their addresses and telephone numbers, for example, Social Services, Social Security, Community Relations, NAYPIC.'

'The guidebook should contain a page each for house rules and pocket money allowances where the young people can fill in their own details as they change from time to time. It would be beneficial for an envelope to be attached to the back of the booklet which could be used for comments on the guide or personal complaints.'

'Finally, all guidebooks should contain Section 18 of the Child Care Act 1980:

In reaching any decision relating to a child in their care a local authority shall give first consideration to the need to safeguard and promote the welfare of the child throughout his childhood; and shall so far as practicable ascertain the wishes and feelings of the child regarding the decision and give due consideration to them having regard to his age and understanding.'

Control or care? Sanitary protection and young women in care

Many young women members of NAYPIC were highly embarrassed by the procedures they had to go through in order to get sanitary protection. It was common practice that they were required to show used sanitary towels to staff in order to get new supplies. This was seen by young women as a way of checking up on them, to see if they were pregnant. Also, they were subject to detailed record keeping of dates when sanitary towels were issued, often causing them extra stress at a time when whey needed it least.

It was these experiences that led to NAYPIC's national survey (1986-1988) of sanitary protection for young women living in residential care.[40] A questionnaire was sent to all Directors of Social Service and Social Work Departments in the United Kingdom to find out how young women in care received sanitary protection and whether as a result of the survey NAYPIC could recommend any improvements in policy and practice.

Local authorities' responses

NAYPIC's survey (just under three quarters of all local authorities responded) revealed that nearly all the authorities (94 per cent) either bulk bought in conjunction with an allowance system (71 per cent) or only issued protection from a bulk bought supply (23 per cent). A very small number of authorities (6 per cent) operated a cash allowance system which gave all the young women in their care the opportunity to be responsible for their sanitary protection.

'Justifications' given by authorities for using bulk buying systems included: the need to have emergency supplies; the age of the young women – some authorities operating dual systems bulk buy and issue protection to younger girls and give an allowance to older girls; the type of establishment - most of the authorities operated dual system bulk buy and issued protection in observation and assessment centres and community homes (education). The survey also found that the allowance systems adopted by authorities also varied and included: young women being given petty cash; young women being given a regular addition to their pocket money; and an allowance being included in a home's 'housekeeping' budget.

NAYPIC found that '*a particularly sensitive nerve for local authorities, as reflected in the relatively low response rate - 44per cent - is the keeping of records.*' Over two-thirds of the authorities who responded kept records of either the issue of sanitary protection or the menstrual cycle or both. Reasons giving for keeping records included: monitoring health; as a pregnancy indicator; to let girls know when they are due, to monitor premenstrual tension (PMT); as a check of the regularity of their periods; to ensure the necessary protection is available; to understand change of moods; to understand behaviour; to note medical infections and irregularity of periods; and, as part of the caring role of staff. Where records weren't kept by the home (in a far fewer number of authorities) reasons included: the importance of encouraging individual responsibility; girls being encouraged to monitor their own cycles and; the keeping records being seen as impeding caring relationships between residential staff and girls.

Young women's views

Although NAYPIC's survey was not primarily aimed at finding out young women's views, it was their experiences that led to the study in the first place. A number of young women surveyed, both members and non members of NAYPIC, wrote to NAYPIC to tell them of their experiences and how they thought practices could be improved:

Cartoons by: Fran Orford

NAYPIC Head Office:
Maranar House, 28-30 Mosley Street, Newcastle NE1 1DF. Tel: 091-261 2178
London Office: 20 Compton Terrace, London N1 2UN. Tel: 01-226 7102

Back cover of Control or Care? Sanitary Protection and Young Women in Care, 1988

'The first children's home I was in was for observation and assessment. We had to ask for sanitary towels and tampons which was quite embarrassing because I hardly knew the staff, and then you were only given ten which sometimes isn't enough so you had to ask again.'

'At this home they have to buy everything in bulk. They send us order forms for everything from County Hall so there is no choice. We all have to use the same toothpaste and Lifeboy B.O. Soap, which we all hate because it smells gross. We've asked if we can have different stuff but County Hall hasn't got anything else on the order form. Tampons and towels are purchased in the same way. We do get a selection but they never seem to buy any 'super' or 'super plus' tampons for heavier girls or even 'slender' for the younger girls.'

'Most of the staff understand that it is embarrassing for us to ask for them so they usually give us big boxes. But they do write it down on a piece of paper attached to the inside of the door to say what you had out of the cupboard and when.'

'In the children's home they wrote it in a book which was supposed to be locked away but I saw it once lying on the side in the medical room where it could have been looked at.'

'As a young person who has been in care, I think young females should be given an allowance, every week they should have a budget on top of their pocket money.'

'The girls shouldn't have to let a member of staff know when their periods start. It's embarrassing because not at all times are there female staff on duty and there are some female staff who young girls can't talk to.'

'There is not enough trust about, surely a girl should be trusted to buy her own sanitary equipment.'

'I think girls should be told about different types of brands. When I was in care I never got told and when I saw different ones I didn't know what to do with them.'

'Why do they keep a record of monthly periods? Surely a young person who has worries would come and let someone know.'

'Why don't assessment units allow girls to buy their own? Girls still have a period whether in short or long stay places. Is it because it doesn't fit in with the staff routine?'

'Young girls and women should be given an allowance so that they can choose - this will be useful as part of becoming independent.'

Policy implications

In discussing the policy implications of its survey, NAYPIC commented:

'The main finding of this survey, in highlighting the extensive use of bulk buying, is the lack of involvement of thousands of young girls and women in care, in the purchase of their own sanitary protection. It is also disturbing to find such an emphasis upon the use of records and by omission so little reference to advice, counselling and education concerning young women's health and sexuality.'

'It would seem from the survey as well as the experience of NAYPIC members and the young women's comments contained within this report, that the system is geared far more to the management and control of what is seen as deviant behaviour by young women - becoming pregnant whilst in care - than to the developing of enabling and trusting relationships between young women and workers. NAYPIC believes that it is only the latter approach that can benefit young women in care and particularly those who find themselves in difficulties.'

It was against this background that NAYPIC agreed the policies outlined below at its Annual General Meeting in 1988.

NAYPIC policy

1. The bulk buying of sanitary products for young people should be abolished.

2. We accept the need for emergency supplies for girls who start periods earlier than expected, or for girls admitted to establishments at short notice. However, emergency supplies can be bought from petty cash at local shops in the community.

3. Young women should be able to seek advice and guidance on menstruation and the menstrual cycle and problems related to the menstrual cycle.

4. Staff should remember at all times to have respect for a young persons' need for privacy.

5. No records should be kept at all unless the young person requests the need for this.

6. We urge local Social Services Department and voluntary child care agencies to draw up a clear policy statement on the issue of sanitary protection and make this widely known to those caring directly for young women.

7. We feel that any policy statements should only be produced after full consultation and involvement of young women in care.

8. We urge local Social Service Departments and voluntary child care agencies to consider giving all young people an extra weekly allowance (or fortnightly) to buy all toiletries, for example, toothpaste, shampoo, shaving cream, deodorants.

9. Adequate facilities for the disposal of waste sanitary products should be provided in all establishments.

'The reason NAYPIC feels strongly about the bulk buying of sanitary protection and toiletries for young people in care is that it does not allow for self-responsibility, privacy nor practical preparation for when a young person looks after themselves when they have left care.'

Evidence to the Review of Residential Care

In 1986, NAYPIC was given another opportunity to directly influence government policy. They were invited to submit evidence to the Wagner Group '*Review of Residential Care*' set up by the Secretary of State for Social Services.[41] In preparing their submission they were able to send the Wagner Group the main publications derived from the work they had undertaken to date, including *Sharing Care*, their charter of rights, and the published reports of their completed surveys. But as well as getting across the views of young people, and their specific policy recommendations contained within these documents, NAYPIC welcomed this chance to convey to the Wagner Group the bigger picture: the importance of young people being more involved in the day-to-day-decisions that shaped their lives.

'In general NAYPIC supports policies and practices that involve young people and encourages them to take greater control over their lives. It is recognised that we need help and assistance from skilled workers in doing this and that we will make mistakes - like young people not in care!'

'NAYPIC is against policies and practices that deny young people opportunities to participate and make them feel different from other young people. We do recognise that learning about life is a gradual process and at times a difficult experience which involves responsibilities to others as well as ourselves. But we do need the opportunities to learn, to make mistakes, to find out about ourselves and others   otherwise we will not be prepared for making our own way in the world. Residential care could have a far more positive image as a key part of community based child care provision.'[42]

NAYPIC also highlighted a number of issues that had arisen from their earlier and ongoing work. This included criticism of the large number of authorities which still operate bulk buying for food, clothes and toiletries and other day-to-day requirements:

'Despite widespread condemnation, the order book arrangement for purchasing clothes still exists in a small number of authorities. Many of the young people we are in contact with are not involved in the planning of menus, or the budgeting, purchasing and preparation of food. The bulk buying of sanitary towels, which does not allow choice of brands, has also recently come to light by a NAYPIC survey.'[43]

NAYPIC also sent the Committee their *Charter of Rights for Young People in Care* that had been agreed at their 1985 *Speak Out Conference*.[44] This extended the earlier *Who Cares Charter* containing seven 'rights,' that NAYPIC had adopted, to a new 100 point charter. It was constructed on the basis of *Sharing Care* as well as the policy issues arising from their campaigns and surveys. It covered six broad areas: files; rules, punishment and discipline; dignity, privacy and personal freedom; proper care; reviews and case conferences; and leaving care and after-care:

*'We recognise that these are not 'rights' in any legally enforceable way but they are all **issues and concerns** that many young people in care feel strongly about. We would like your committee to read them – for they have arisen from our meetings with young people in care. What they add up to is how NAYPIC sees the*

'We need help and assistance from skilled workers'

responsibilities and duties of a substitute caring parent. We recognise that they are ideals, that some of them need more working out and that there will be the need for compromise and flexibility: but nevertheless they represent many of the important issues for us as consumers of care.'[45]

Another topic raised by NAYPIC in their evidence to the Wagner Group was the use of assessment centres and large children's homes, including community homes with education on site. The experience of NAYPIC's members was that young people spent too long being assessed, and often felt they had been 'dumped'. They were also concerned that these institutions were too far away from young people's families, and that they were being assessed in an artificial and unusual atmosphere:

*'NAYPIC believes that young people who cannot live at home should be assessed in children's homes, foster care, or perhaps by a day care centre linked with the homes. We also think there is too much **individual assessment**. Couldn't there be more attempts to assess whole families? Many of the same criticisms apply to community homes with education. NAYPIC members find them too large, too remote and too institutional to help young people. We believe that most young people, even if they are very upset or experiencing severe difficulties, can be helped in small homes given well qualified staff and good staffing levels.'*[46]

Also, in their evidence, NAYPIC members commented on the great variation in the quality of care they received:

'Should the government play a greater role in achieving better standards of care? Also, where there are differences within areas should there be stronger and better trained management to get rid of bad practices. NAYPIC also believes that it should be standard practice for young people to be seen and their views taken into account when homes are visited by inspectors or central office staff. This rarely happens at the present time which means 'outsiders' only have a partial view of what is going on within a home.'[47]

NAYPIC members wanted children's homes to have a far more positive image. Their evidence continued:

'Homes could become more widely used as neighbourhood resources, e.g. when young people need 'time out' of a family for a short period. The main official

attitude should not be to keep young people out of care at all costs. This very negative view contributes to the stigma of care as a 'bad' last resort... children's homes could develop far more positive links with neighbourhoods and offer a system of shared care to families at times of difficulty.'[48]

NAYPIC members also advocated to the Wagner Group that a complaints system should be available to all young people in care, linked to greater opportunities for participation. They restated their position from *Sharing Care*, their 1983 evidence to the House of Commons Committee on Children in Care:

'NAYPIC supports proposals for a new and independent complaints procedure. However, this cannot be done in isolation. Young people need to be more involved in the running of their home and we feel that a complaints procedure should fit into an overall commitment to allowing young people to voice their feelings and opinions and for them to see that suggestions and complaints will be acted upon. A formal complaints system would not then be the only form for redress. And many smaller cases or incidents would not have to go through a lengthy and complicated procedure.'[49]

Finally, in their evidence, NAYPIC, argued for *'better preparation whilst young people are in care and better support and assistance for young people after they leave.'*

NAYPIC meets its aims

NAYPIC's reports reached a wide audience. They were sent to all local authorities in the UK and discussed at regional and national conferences. Also, NAYPIC's workers were invited by some social service department's senior managers to help them introduce the policy recommendations contained within their survey reports. Their survey work also led to both NAYPIC staff and, importantly, members of local in care groups becoming involved in training social services staff.

There was a high degree of optimism among NAYPIC staff and members that they were successfully *'promoting the views and opinions of young people in care'* and *'improving conditions for children and young people in care,'* two of the main aims of NAYPIC, as defined in their constitution. They were also convinced that their views mattered, not only to local authorities but also to government itself.

NAYPIC's 1986 evidence to the Wagner Group's *Review of Residential Care* continued to show the overall poor state of care experienced by many young people – echoing the main findings in their 1983 evidence to the Social Services

Committee, *Sharing Care*. They expressed particular concerns about the lack of opportunities for young people to participate in the decisions which shaped their lives, including their reviews. Many of the young people they surveyed felt they were poorly prepared for leaving care, and inadequately supported after they left care. Young people were also critical of the large number of authorities which still operated bulk buying for food, clothes and toiletries and other day-to-day requirements – even though these concerns had first been raised in 1973!

However, despite the success of their surveys, and their work at a local and national level, all was not well within the organisation. Trouble was brewing.

Chapter 9

NAYPIC's troubles

'NAYPIC had high expectations that their funding application would be successful – a formality - given what they had achieved so far, and how highly their work was regarded by a wide range of statutory and voluntary organisations, including both central and local government.'

NAYPIC's complicated organisational arrangements

NAYPIC's achievements between 1979 and 1988 were impressive. This was the more so, in that from its inception in 1979 to 1983, when it received its first funding from the government, its activities were sustained by the voluntary efforts of a small group of young people who had grown up in care. It was they who led the organisation during these years.

In order to secure its first government grant in 1983, NAYPIC's organisational arrangements were complex and potentially divisive. Because the organisation had failed to secure charitable status, its grant was administered through another voluntary organisation, the National Council for Voluntary Organisations (NCVO). This arrangement not only denied NAYPIC direct control of their own finances, but also resulted in them having to set up the In Care Company, in order to pursue charitable status. The organisational arrangements were further complicated as it was a condition of receiving their government grant that an Adult Advisory Group be set up, as a separate group from the Young Person's National Steering Group. However, despite the complexities and the potential for conflict, these arrangements hung together quite well during the first two years of funding. But from 1985 onwards significant difficulties and tensions developed.

In August 1985, the London Boroughs Grant Unit (LBGU), the replacement grant awarding arm of the defunct Greater London Council, funded two workers and a new London office of NAYPIC. This was good news. It provided an opportunity to develop NAYPIC's much needed work in the capital. However, it also, potentially, added to the organisational complexities. The London office of NAYPIC was organisationally and financially independent of 'national' NAYPIC. This was not to prove a problem during the first year of the grant, as the London office and NAYPIC closely co-ordinated their activities. After all, securing funding for the London office was seen as a 'success' for NAYPIC's track record to date.

More government funding – a formality?

In March 1986, NAYPIC applied for a further three years of government funding, to follow on from the initial grant aid, which was due to end in July 1986. They had high expectations that this would be successful - a formality given what they had achieved so far, and how highly their work was regarded by a wide range of statutory and voluntary organisations, including both central and local government. As a member of their steering group had remarked, '*NAYPIC's campaigns were succeeding in lightening the load for young people still in care and leaving care*'.

In this context, NAYPIC saw the grant application as an opportunity for expansion, by opening a new office in the Midlands. This would give them a North, South and a new Midlands presence, as well as an opportunity to build on their established and well respected work programme and expertise.

However, despite making numerous inquiries about their grant application, they had heard nothing from the government by the end of July 1986, by which time their funding had run out. The three full-time workers, one based in the London national NAYPIC office (not the new London branch office) and two in the Bradford office, were laid off at the end of their contracts. However, their commitment to NAYPIC and 'the cause' led them to continue their work, all be it in a voluntary capacity, and as their office leases had not yet expired, at least they had a place of work to go to.

On 15 September 1986, two months after their grant had ended, they received a formal response to their funding application from the Department of Health and Social Security (referred to as the department). It stated that there were '*some difficulties with the application, to be clarified before further payment of a grant can be made*'. This included '*the need for clear organisational responsibility and accountability for the grant – the present organisational arrangements were very unclear between NAYPIC (who carried out day-to-day activities) NCVO (who*

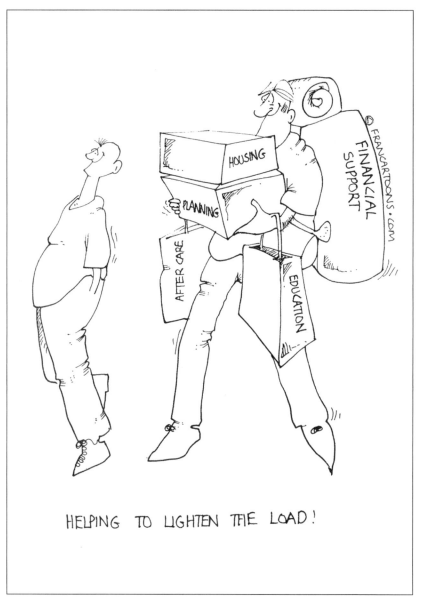

'NAYPIC's campaigns were lightening the load for young people still in care and leaving care'

administered the grant) and the In Care Company (that existed but was not active).' The letter also stipulated that the department wanted NAYPIC to seek a proportion of its income from other sources, and to agree specific programme objectives and targets with NAYPIC. They proposed that their representatives meet with NAYPIC to discuss the difficulties they had identified, as well as the possibility of some interim funding.[50]

In respect of the latter, NAYPIC wrote immediately to the department spelling out the problems caused by the delay in funding: the absence of paid staff to maintain the volume and high quality of the work carried out during the period of the original grant, and the impact on NAYPIC's credibility if it were to '*shut up shop*' for any length of time. In response to NAYPIC's letter, the department agreed to meet with them on 21 October 1986 to discuss the issues raised. In preparation for that meeting, NAYPIC provided the department with their proposals to amend the organisational arrangements at their 1986 November Annual General Meeting (AGM), in order that they could receive and administer their own grant.

At the meeting on 21 October, the department representative restated the need for NAYPIC to become formally constituted as a voluntary organisation in their own right, and to be directly responsible and accountable for grant aid, possibly through the In Care Company having charitable status. They also re-stated their requirement for a more structured work plan with specific targets. However, they did agree to give NAYPIC a small interim grant (£2,850) to cover the Bradford office rent, as well as the costs associated with their planned AGM, and meetings of the management group, the professional support group, and the meeting with the department. But there was to be no funding for the three full-time posts. The staff who had been laid off were expected to continue working in a voluntary capacity.

The Birmingham Annual General Meeting

As planned, NAYPIC's AGM was held at the Birmingham Council House on 19 November 1986. The proposed constitutional and organisational changes, critical to securing future departmental funding, were discussed. But there was to be no immediate resolution. It was decided by the meeting to delay voting on these proposals. It was agreed by a majority vote that further discussion by the membership and regional management groups were needed. This would allow fuller documentation of the proposed changes to be prepared for the next AGM in 1987.'

However, important decisions *were* voted on. It was agreed to move the Northern office from Bradford to Newcastle, to maintain the London office, and if funding were available, have a Midlands and Southern Office. Also, a range of equal opportunities policies were approved, including a proposal that NAYPIC's logo should have an image of a black young person. It was also agreed that membership should continue to be free to young people until the next AGM, and that discussions should continue with the National Children's Bureau about producing a joint *NAYPIC and Who Cares?* newsletter instead of having two separate publications. In respect of these proposals much was achieved at the AGM. But the process was very difficult, mainly as a consequence of a major split between the London representatives and the other regional representatives on many of the issues discussed, resulting at one stage in a 'walk out'. The reasons for the split were several: genuine differences of opinion on key issues; how these were expressed, and; some personality clashes. But the withholding of funding was not in any way conducive to constructive debate. Nevertheless, the meeting just held together to progress the issues detailed above, although it was evident to all that a chasm had opened up.

After the AGM, the relationship between the London group and the Professional Advisory Group (PAG) broke down when the contents of a confidential letter from a member of the PAG to other members, reflecting on the conduct of the AGM, was leaked and seen as an attack on the behaviour of the London group and its representatives. However, despite the lack of funding, and these major organisational difficulties, NAYPIC's funded staff in London and volunteer workers in Bradford continued to carry out work at both local and national levels.

Restoration of government funding

It wasn't until 26 January 1987, six months after the end of their initial funding, that the department wrote to NAYPIC agreeing to continue funding them.[51] They were to receive grant aid for a 15 month period, from January 1987 to 31 March 1988, not the three-year grant they had requested. There was to be no back dating of staffing costs, and no financial recognition of the hardship caused to NAYPIC or the three staff who were laid off but had continued to work in a voluntary capacity.

In securing the grant, NAYPIC agreed with the department to carry out a work programme with local authorities on: guides for young people in care; preparation for leaving care; and involving young people in care in child care training programmes. NAYPIC also agreed with the department that it would hold a conference for local councillors and publish its survey findings on '*guides for young people in care and sanitary protection and young women in care*'.

Finally, the department, in their letter, 'accepted' that NAYPIC was progressing its constitutional and organisational reforms, and agreed that until *'satisfactory arrangements can be concluded'* (at the next AGM) the National Council for Voluntary Organisations (NCVO) would continue to administer NAYPIC's grant.

At the beginning of June 1987, NAYPIC received a follow up letter asking what progress had been made on their organisational reforms and making it clear that *'further funding will depend, among other things, on NAYPIC's ability to show that it has carried out the work programme for which the grant was given and has proper control of its income and expenditure'.*[52]

Organisational changes

On 10 June 1987 a special meeting of the Professional Advisory Group (PAG) was held to look at the roles and responsibilities of the group in relation to NAYPIC. More specifically, the meeting discussed how to respond to the department's letter in order to ensure that the work programme was carried out, and address the organisational issues raised in the letter. Faced with the possible future loss of the departmental grant, the PAG agreed to set up a National Steering Group (NSG) constituted by representatives drawn from current members of NAYPIC, members of the PAG and former NAYPIC workers (who by NAYPIC's constitution had to step down when they reached 25 years of age). The members of PAG also agreed that the group would be chaired by a former civil servant with substantial administrative experience, and that he would undertake a review of the present organisational difficulties.

His review, set in the context of NAYPIC's substantial achievements, suggested that there should be an Interim National Steering Group, responsible for the direction of the work of NAYPIC on behalf of its membership.[53] This would include oversight of the grant expenditure and the attainment of the work programme specified by the department. The proposed membership of the group was: five members from the PAG; two associate members of NAYPIC (from workers or former members who had reached 25); and two representatives from each of the three regional NAYPIC management committees.

The proposals were discussed at the first meeting of the Interim National Steering Group on 13 July 1987. After much discussion and disagreement - one NAYPIC member resigned - it was agreed that the interim group would continue until 31 March 1988. It would address organisational issues and progress the work programme to ensure continuation of departmental funding, and then hand over to NAYPIC. It was agreed that the chair of the NSG would act as chair of the interim steering group.

Three meetings of the interim NSG were held during the remainder of 1987 (on 3 September; 29 October and 3 December). The uneasy consensus that had emerged at the initial meeting did not last long. The London and Southern representatives viewed the NSG as 'unconstitutional' and wanted to increase the voting representation of young people from the regional management groups. This was opposed by representatives from the North region, resulting in a north south divide. However, despite these tensions, the NSG continued to meet. It was agreed that the NSG should prepare a report to the department on the work being carried out by NAYPIC and the regional groups, as well as the planning taking place for the next AGM.

On the 16 December 1987, the department met with the six NAYPIC development workers (two from the south; two from London; and two from the North) to discuss funding from March 1988 when their existing grant was due to end. The department made it clear that future funding would be dependent on: audited accounts for 1987-1988; reports of the work carried out; receiving the accounts of the In Care Company, and whether it was in a position to take over the administration of the grant. They requested to receive this information by 31 January 1988.

Seeking further government funding

At the National Steering Group meeting on 7 January 1988, the chair agreed to prepare the funding application for a further two years (1 April 1988-31 March 1990). This was submitted to the department by the end of January 1988, as requested, detailing the work undertaken on guidebooks for children in care, preparation for leaving care and the involvement of young people in care in the training of social workers. It also made it clear that the NSG was intending to revive the In Care Company as the organisation to which the grant would be payable, given NAYPIC's lack of charitable status. As regard future work, the application to the department outlined NAYPIC's plans to build upon three main areas: guidebooks, leaving care and training. Finally, NAYPIC informed the department that it would strengthen its organisation by establishing and maintaining more local 'in care' groups:

'To this end NAYPIC hopes to be able to convince all local authorities that they should enrol, and pay a subscription to NAYPIC for all children and young people in their care in a similar way to the subscriptions paid for students to the National Union of Students.'[54]

This would also enable NAYPIC to establish an alternative source of funding, another stipulation of the department.

On 21 June 1988, NAYPIC received a letter from the department confirming that they had been successful in their grant application and would be funded from 1 April 1988 to 31 March 1990, to carry out the programme of work outlined in the application.[55] A condition of the grant was that NAYPIC would '*try to substantially increase its income from non-DHSS sources in order to become more self-supporting in the long term.*' The grant would continue to be paid through the NCVO until the In Care Company was able to take over the funding. The department also wanted to hold a series of ongoing meetings with NAYPIC representatives to review progress.

The first of these meetings was held on 6 October 1988 with representatives of the department and the National Steering Group. The internal tensions within NAYPIC and the NSG had become evident to the department through their representative on the NSG (from the Professional Advisory Group) and were discussed at that meeting. Following the meeting the department wrote to NAYPIC raising serious concerns about the organisational structure.[56] This included:

- '*Strained and blurred*' relationships between the Professional Advisory Group, the National Steering Group, the North and South management groups and NAYPIC's AGM.

- NAYPIC not having a recognised membership scheme – '*until this is resolved, it is difficult to see how meetings such as the AGM where major decisions are reached can properly be said to be reflecting the views of members.*'

- The need to clarify the role of the regional management committees and their relationship with the NSG.

- Clarification of the role of the In Care Company if it is to take over from the NSG including its responsibilities, the procedures by which its directors are appointed, its relationship with the local management committees and the AGM.

On 28 October 1988 a meeting was held with representatives of NAYPIC's National Steering Group, the In Care Company and the department to respond to these issues. At that meeting it was agreed:[57]

- The In Care Company would become operational by the end of 1988.

- The nine In Care Company director posts would be filled by three posts appointed by the company; three ex-care representatives; and three nominees by NAYPIC (elected at the AGM).

- These arrangements would be '*of an interim nature and designed to provide a degree of stability which is essential if NAYPIC is to continue to receive central government funding. The longer term objective remains for the In Care Company, as far as is practicable, to be organised and run by young people themselves.*'

- Future payments of the grant (from January 1989) would be dependent on confirmation, no later than 31 December 1988, that the new structure of the In Care Company is in place and in operation.

On 19 December 1988 the secretary of the In Care Company wrote to the department confirming that the organisational arrangements agreed above had been made, although they wished to delay the transfer of grant aid to the ICC until they had appointed a finance officer to administer the grant. A letter was also sent to the London Borough Grants Unit (LBGU), which was responsible for funding a post in London, informing them of the changes and inviting them to the first meeting of the In Care Company.

The In Care Company

The first meeting of the newly formed In Care Company was held on 20 January 1989 and confirmed its directors in post (six young people who had been in care and three adult supporters). The ICC was to have responsibility for employing four staff, who no longer had to be under 25 years of age; drawing up and agreeing work programmes; and approving funding applications on behalf on NAYPIC. It was also agreed at the meeting that the Northern office should be moved from Newcastle (which had not operated for some time) to Manchester, and that a new membership scheme should be introduced. A NAYPIC conference was to be planned for the summer of 1989 to agree policies. Representatives from the Department of Health and the London Borough Grant Unit attended part of the meeting to receive feedback on the plans.

Following this meeting, a letter was received from the London Boroughs Grants Scheme representative expressing three major concerns: first, that only three members of the In Care Company were current members of NAYPIC; second, the lack of agreement about the role of the In Care Company in managing NAYPIC; and third, the failure to have a detailed plan and timetable to hand back control to NAYPIC. The LBGU also made it clear that it would continue to fund and support the London office and worker until these issues were resolved and saw '*no need for the In Care Company to be involved in any way with the current London activities*'⁵⁸.

Government grant suspended

The rejection by London NAYPIC of the proposals agreed by NAYPIC's National Steering Group and the In Care Company with the Department of Health was to have an immediate impact. Despite receiving revised organisational arrangements from NAYPIC (as detailed above) the department suspended grant payments from January 1989 citing the separate funding and organisational arrangements developing between the In Care Company and London NAYPIC (part funded by the LBGU).⁵⁹ For a second time in its short history NAYPIC was faced with a funding crisis. Their paid workers, young people from care who had overcome a lot in their lives and given a lot to NAYPIC, found themselves unemployed once again. NAYPIC wrote to the department highlighting the disastrous impact of the suspension of the grant on its work '*as a respected national organisation.*'

'*Because the grant has been suspended the workers employed by NAYPIC have either resigned or have had their employment terminated. While a London office does remain it is staffed and run through the grant from the London Boroughs Grant Unit which limits its scope to London matters only.*'⁶⁰

However, the department was not to be moved. On 20 April 1989, they wrote to the secretary of the In Care Company informing NAYPIC that the grant will remain suspended. They commented:

'*There appears to be a possibility that there might well be two separate organisations operating under the banner of 'NAYPIC'. If this were to become the case we would regard it as particularly unfortunate and could lead to potential confusion. I am sure you would share our view that NAYPIC should be seen as a 'national' organisation which represents the views of all children in care to both central and local government. We hope therefore that you will continue to attempt to reach an accommodation with the LBGU to achieve these objectives.*'⁶¹

The letter made it clear that 'to lift the suspension of the grant' the following information would be required:⁶²

• *A statement of the In Care Company's future aims and objectives for*

NAYPIC including the arrangements for the appointment of directors and the company secretary (with a job description).

- *The management arrangements for the North and South offices including the appointment of the management committees, their roles and functions, and relationship with the Company.*

- *A timetable for the setting up of the North and South offices and the recruitment of staff.*

- *A timetable for generating membership and how it is proposed this will be achieved.*

- *A timetable for an Annual General Meeting to re-launch NAYPIC.*

On 26 June the secretary of the In Care Company responded to these points, as detailed below:

- The In Care Company would aim to be responsible for the employment of all NAYPIC staff – '*not just Department of Health funded posts.*' The In Care Company board would also replace the previous North and South management committees.

- A new office would be set up in Manchester replacing Newcastle in the North, and the London office in the South (that was now independently funded and operated by the London Boroughs Grants Unit). The Manchester office would also '*for the time being cover national interests. At some later date hopefully a London based office (with workers funded by the London Boroughs grant and from the department grant) can be set up.*'

- A National Conference, *Speak Out 89* was planned for the end of August to re-establish NAYPIC. The details had been circulated to all Directors of Social Services asking them to invite three young people and one adult. The delegates would be asked to join NAYPIC as members, vote in a new constitution and elect three young people to the Company's board

Also, in their response, NAYPIC requested the department to re-instate the grant for three workers for the Manchester office, but not at this time funding for a London post - thus their grant application was proportionally three-quarters of that originally approved.

Government grant restored

On 7 August 1989 the department wrote to NAYPIC agreeing to reinstate the grant from August 1989 to 31 March 1990, the end of the original grant period. As on the previous occasion when NAYPIC's funding was cut, there was to be no back payment, or recompense to NAYPIC to cover the seven month gap in funding. Also, in restoring the grant, the department also re-stated its concern at the split between the London office, funded by the LBGU, and NAYPIC.

*'We look to NAYPIC to be a **national** organisation representing the views and interests of children in care wherever they may be. We would urge therefore that further efforts should be made as quickly as possible to reach a flexible accommodation with the London office and their Management Committee to ensure that NAYPIC remains a truly national organisation. Their interest and participation in the national conference later this month should also not be over looked.'*

The letter concluded:

'We hope you have a successful national conference at the end of the month and that it achieves its objective of publicly re-establishing NAYPIC as a national voice for children in care'.[63]

Chapter 10

Speak Out '89 - A new beginning?

'We went outside the door and held banners saying 'warning this is not a NAYPIC conference'. We handed out leaflets to young people saying 'Urgent Notice' explaining the situation.'

(London members picketing Speak Out '89 conference)

Speak Out 89 was to hold the key to NAYPIC's destiny. The Department of Health, its main funding body, saw it as an opportunity to re-launch NAYPIC as a *national* organisation, uniting the warring London and 'national' NAYPIC offices. For the In Care Company it provided the opportunity to show that it could be a unifying force, both organisationally and financially. And for NAYPIC itself, it was an opportunity for a new beginning, to win the support of the local authorities, and, most importantly, the minds of young people in their care.

NAYPIC, Children's rights and the Children Act 1989

Although NAYPIC's future was clouded in uncertainty, their contribution to the wider 'children's rights' agenda had been far reaching. In November 1989 the new Children Act was to be introduced. Its journey had begun with the 1984 House of Commons Committee Report on Children in Care, and the impact of NAYPIC's evidence, *Sharing Care*, had been explicitly acknowledged in their report. NAYPIC's contribution was recognised both at a general level, of the need to listen to the views of young people - referred to in their Parliamentary Report as 'children's rights' - and in their specific recommendations in respect of attendance at reviews, leaving care, and the need for young people to have a complaints procedure.

NAYPIC also maintained the 'children's rights' momentum through their published surveys and in their evidence to the Wagner Committee's Review of Residential Care, as discussed in Chapters 7 and 8. NAYPIC was recognised by government and senior policy makers not only as a key player in the children's rights lobby but as the only 'consumer' group for young people in care, giving the organisation a high degree of legitimacy.

During the same period, 'adult' professional pressure groups such as the Children's Legal Centre and A Voice for the Child in Care were also advocating for the greater involvement of children and young people in decision making. There was also evidence of change at a local level. The first children's rights officer in the UK was appointed by Leicestershire in 1987 and a small number of local authorities introduced complaints procedures for young people in care. But these were very much the exceptions. Most local authorities did not have complaints procedures by 1989 and in this regard they had ignored NAYPIC's views and the implications of the Kincora and Leeways Inquiries into the abuse of young people living in children's homes, both published in 1985.[64]

For those campaigning for children to be given equal rights to adults - far more than merely 'consulting' children, the ruling of the House of Lords in the Victoria Gillick case, to uphold the right of doctors to prescribe contraception to young people under 16 without parental consent, was seen as a significant victory. The Children's Legal Centre issued a briefing devoted to the House of Lords Ruling in which it commented:

'First and foremost the Gillick decision is a landmark for the rights of children. It is the first legal judgement which unequivocally recognises the right of young people to make decisions about their lives and their bodies. The Victorian concept of absolute parental authority and control has been replaced by the new concept of partnership between parents and children. The power of the parent dwindles and the power of the child increases as the child grows in years and understanding.'[65]

There were also important developments on the international stage. Most significantly, the United Nations Convention on the Rights of the Child was due to be adopted in November 1989 (although not to be ratified by the UK until 1991), including the landmark Article 12, recognising for the first time the human rights of children as individuals in their own right, including the right of children to participate in all decisions that affect them. [66]

'NAYPIC's contribution to the children's rights agenda had been far reaching'

It was against this background that the Children Act 1989 enhanced the rights of children and young people in the welfare arena. Under the new Act, their '*wishes and feelings*' were to be considered by the courts, as well as in making decisions about them in care or accommodation. Local authorities were also required to '*give due consideration to the child's religious persuasion, racial origin, culture and language*'. They were also for the first time required to establish complaints procedures including '*an independent element*' and publish information about services. The Act also strengthened leaving care legislation by a new duty to prepare young people for independence, and the extension of permissive powers '*to advise and befriend*' wider groups of young people. Also, for the first time, young people aged 16-21 were able to request that the local authority provide them with accommodation.

These legal changes had been greatly influenced by NAYPIC's activities, including *Sharing Care* - their evidence to the House of Commons, their surveys and their campaigning activities. It was ironic that as the 1989 Act was passed, NAYPIC's own future hung in the balance.

Speak Out 89 – a new beginning?

Speak Out 89 was held at the Hayes Conference Centre in Derbyshire between Wednesday 30 August and Friday 1 September 1989. All local authorities in England were invited to send three young people in care aged between 13 and 18, and one adult to accompany them. But although *Speak Out* was planned as an event to unify the different NAYPIC factions, the full-time London worker, funded by the London Borough's Grant Unit, and members of the London branch, were not invited. In fact, they had only found out about *Speak Out*, as well as the news about the restoration of the government's grant to NAYPIC, which did not include re-instating the grant funding for a 'national' NAYPIC London worker, on 3 August in *Community Care* magazine.[67] They were incandescent!

The London worker approached the secretary of the In Care Company the day before the conference asking if the London branch of NAYPIC could attend but they were refused permission. Following a meeting of the London management committee, and having sought legal advice, it was agreed that their worker and two members of the London committee would attend the conference and deliver a solicitor's letter to the In Care Company. This would inform them that as *Speak Out 89* was not a NAYPIC event but an In Care Company conference any changes to NAYPIC's constitution would have no legal grounds.

As had been agreed by the management committee, the three London members arrived on the Wednesday, the first morning of *Speak Out 89*, only to be told by the chair, secretary and an adult director of the In Care Company that that they could not attend. The London worker responded: '*You leave us no other alternative than to picket the conference*' and then handed them the solicitor's letter.

'We went outside the doors and held banners saying '**Warning – this is not a NAYPIC conference.**' *We handed out leaflets to young people saying* '*Urgent Notice*' *explaining the situation to them.'*

The representatives of the In Care Company came outside and again asked them to leave which they refused to do. They then called the police who escorted the London members to the gate.

'They (the police) said we could picket there so long as we didn't go onto the premises. We continued handing out leaflets to cars of people arriving at the conference. During the day young people kept coming down to see us and tell us what they were saying at the conference. By 5.30 pm we had about 40 or more young people down at the gate. We decided to hold our own meeting and wrote down 32 issues young people wanted to have a conference about. Support was growing, there were about 70 young people demanding that we speak at the conference.'

Faced with the growing support for the London delegates and a possible rebellion by young people, the conference organisers agreed that the London worker could address the conference to explain her position. The worker welcomed this opportunity and told the young people that the proposed constitution of the In Care Company, by only having three NAYPIC representatives (young people in or ex care under 25) out of nine members, represented a 'takeover' of NAYPIC by the ICC, and that it should be resisted at all costs.

'I explained the situation with the In Care Company and young people were outraged at the takeover and demanded that the ICC come to the conference hall and explain themselves. We took a break for about 20 minutes and the two sides met again with all the delegates and adults present. Young people started arguing with adults and the ICC demanding that they hold a vote. In the end young people decided to chuck the adults out of the room and make a decision themselves. I said I would also go out of the room.'

'We stood outside and heard an almighty cheer. Then the doors bust open and young people were hugging and kissing each other. They had decided that the

ICC should have three young people in care on the board together with three young people ex-care under 25 years old and three adults of their choice.'

Following this change to the In Care Company constitution, returning the majority voting power to NAYPIC - young people in care and ex care under 25 years of age - there were celebrations on Wednesday evening. A lot of alcohol was consumed. There were a lot of drunken and sick young people, and accusations were made that this had been provoked by the London delegates. They strongly denied this. But it provided the organisers of Speak Out with an excuse to evict the London group. On the following morning delegates were in the conference hall at 9am.

'One of the organisers stood at the front and said: 'Right, we have had a meeting with the conference staff and we will be having a vote. There will be no discussion about it. The vote is, either the London worker and delegates leave, or we will cancel the conference'. About 40 people voted for us to leave but the majority abstained. We stood up, said nothing and left the conference.'

'We were calling a cab at the foyer when we discovered that many of the delegates were following us out, saying that what had been done was wrong. We were walking down the drive when young people told us that the ICC was cancelling the conference and that the organisers had decided to make the remaining delegates (which were few) instant free members in order to vote the ICC version of the new NAYPIC constitution through. This basically gives the ICC the power to administer NAYPIC.'

The Wednesday evening vote taken by young people on the membership of the ICC had been overturned. NAYPIC members, young people under the age of 25 from care backgrounds were no longer to be in a majority on the ICC National Steering Group. Greatly angered by this 'invalid' decision the London worker said that the 'real NAYPIC' would hold its own AGM. It was planned on 26 October 1989.

'At the AGM we hope to create a sound structural basis so that young people can run their own organisation, and so that this kind of attempt to take us over will not happen again. If our conference is successful we will fight to get the Department of Health money back from the ICC so that NAYPIC can continue being the organisation that is a platform for young people in care to speak out.'

But what would be the reaction of those who had such high hopes riding on Speak Out 1989?

Chapter 11

The aftermath

'*NAYPIC RELAUNCH ENDS IN CONFERENCE CHAOS*'

(Community Care, 7 September 1989)

The high expectations riding on *Speak Out 89* to secure NAYPIC's future had come to nought. The split between the London NAYPIC delegates and the officials of the In Care Company, and how this was played out at *Speak Out 89*, was covered in all the press reports the following week. Community Care, the magazine most widely read by social workers and residential staff, highlighted the 'chaos' enveloping the event.[68] They cited the views of a residential and day care officer from Leeds who attended the conference with three young people.[69]

'*Not one of the issues for young people in care was taken up – it was completely disrupted by the split among delegates.*'

However, in the immediate aftermath, concern about the split and the possible demise of NAYPIC led the Director of Social Services for Newcastle to propose that the Association of Directors of Social Services (ADSS), the British Association of Social Workers (BASW) and the Social Care Association (SCA) should join forces to help heal the rift. His view was clear:

'*We cannot afford to have an organisation which represents some of the most vulnerable people in our organisations falling apart.*'[70]

But there was to be no immediate end to hostilities. On 26 October 1989, the London branch of NAYPIC held its '*Real NAYPIC*' conference at a church hall in Islington.

A lot of hard work and forward planning had gone into this meeting, in order to hold elections and agree a new structure for the organisation, independent of the In Care Company. In the event it was also to prove a disaster. Only 25 delegates turned up. '*NAYPIC INDEPENDENCE DAY FLOPS*' proclaimed *Social Work Today* in a report from 2 November 1989. The report continued, '*the failure of its conference now leaves the future of the London organisation in doubt.*'[71]

The In Care Company applies for government funding

It was against this background, including the failure of *Speak Out 89* to unify NAYPIC, as well as the continued strife between the London branch and the In Care Company, that the In Care Company pressed ahead with its application for funding to the Department of Health. The current grant was due to expire on 31 March 1990 and the ICC applied for three year funding to continue their core activities and set up a membership data base. On 12 March 1990 they received a letter from the department rejecting their application.

'*The continued internal divisions within NAYPIC do not, at present, make it possible to approve even core funding. We appreciate the amount of work done by the In Care Company and NAYPIC to introduce better financial control and management arrangements. However, NAYPIC is still internally divided between the In Care Company/NAYPIC and the NAYPIC London/South office and is, therefore, unable to operate as a fully national organisation representing the views and interests of children in care. It is absolutely essential for these two groups within NAYPIC to unite, to agree on future financial, management and staffing arrangements, and to work as one organisation, before the department can consider giving further funding to NAYPIC.*'[72]

The refusal of the grant was also covered widely in the social work press. This initially reinforced the divisions between London NAYPIC which continued to receive LBGU funding and the In Care Company. Under the headline 'A long drawn out battle relentlessly waged', Community Care reported:

'*The London branch of NAYPIC is simultaneously delighted and furious that the ICC has again come financially unstuck, because it believes it should have received the grant. The internecine feud between those two offices has caught the social services press headlines, clouding the real purpose of a national body. The feud has revolved around the issue of who should get the Department of Health grant and thereby effectively run NAYPIC.*'[73]

Abuse in Care

But London NAYPIC also continued its activities. In April 1990 it published a report of *Abuse in the Care System, a pilot study* based upon interviews with 50 young people who contacted them within a three month period.

'*The findings in our research were staggering, with 65 per cent of all young people interviewed having been sexually abused whilst in care, and 75 per cent of young people interviewed having been physically abused. Very few of the young people interviewed were believed when they had complained, most had not complained because they either did not think they would be believed or were too frightened to complain. Even when young people were believed, the police were seldom involved, prosecutions were rare, and even disciplinary action was rarely taken – the person concerned often resigned or took early retirement or either party was moved to another home.*'[74]

The findings from London NAYPIC's abuse survey were reported in the social work press. But like the earlier revelations of such abuses of young people in care, from the *Who Cares?* project in the 1970's and NAYPIC's *Life in Care* conference in 1981, there was to be no political, public or professional outcry for action to be taken, an issue I will return to in my concluding chapter.

Pressure to restore NAYPIC's government funding

NAYPIC's loss of funding led to sustained professional and political pressure to restore the grant and secure NAYPIC's future. The Association of Directors of Social Services wrote to the Department of Health's chief civil servant, the Permanent Secretary, asking him to reverse the decision to refuse the organisation's grant. There was also pressure from the Department of Health and the ADSS for London NAYPIC and the In Care Company to resolve their difficulties if they were going to secure future funding. The pressure applied by these powerful groups paid off. During the autumn of 1990, London NAYPIC and the ICC development worker, met to work out their differences and prepare a joint funding application to the Department of Health. This was submitted on 14 December. The application stated:

'*The past differences between NAYPIC and the In Care Company have now been resolved. NAYPIC is now officially run by under 25's in and ex-care as originally set out in its constitution. The In Care Company will have its charitable status and company status dissolved. It will no longer be known as the In Care*

Company. NAYPIC's national executive will register as a company limited by guarantee whose role will be to receive monies and employ workers.' [75]

The new funding application was to establish and staff offices in four English regions: the North East, the North West, the Midlands, the South East, as well as one in Wales. The workers would be employed by NAYPIC's national executive and be accountable to the management committees in each of the regions. The London Management Committee and workers (funded by the LBGU) would be fully integrated within this structure. Policy would be decided at the Annual General Meeting.

The work objectives identified in the application were to:

'achieve a majority representation of young people in and ex-care affiliated to the association; a forum that would be nationally recognised as being able to provide the opportunity for young people to represent themselves at all levels of decision making and political processes, and which would have a direct effect on their lives whist in and ex care. It was also planned that the organisation would provide young people with knowledge of their rights and ensure they were upheld; provide a comprehensive wide ranging service which would provide educational material for professionals and the general public to assist them in their understanding of the issues related to young people in and ex care'; and finally, to continue the development of consumer orientated services which would achieve NAYPIC's primary objective 'simply to give young people in and ex care a voice.' [76]

Following the submission of their funding application in December 1990, representatives of NAYPIC met with Department of Health civil servants in May, June and July 1991 to discuss their proposed work programme. At the June meeting they also met with Virginia Bottomley, then Minister of State for Health. It was evident from this meeting that high level political and professional pressure had been building up to restore grant aid to NAYPIC.

On 12 August 1991, NAYPIC was informed that its grant application for three years, from 1 October 1991 to 31 March 1994 had been approved, *'to enable NAYPIC to provide a service helping local statutory and voluntary agencies directly helping young people in care, and to enable NAYPIC to represent the views and experience of young people in care at both local and national levels.'* [77]

'NAYPIC's objective, simply to give young people in and ex-care a voice'

In a letter to NAYPIC, the Department of Health stated:[78]

- *The grant is to be used to meet the national administration costs of NAYPIC and the costs of establishing and running offices in three regions of England, namely the North West, the North East and the South East.*

- *The department would also make a 'start up' grant to NAYPIC, before the start of the main grant period, to enable membership packs to be produced and arrangements made for the Annual General Meeting.*

- *Grant-aid will be paid initially through the National Council of Voluntary Organisations (NCVO). We also note that, as part of the reorganisation of NAYPIC, it is intended that the In Care Company is to be wound up and that NAYPIC will seek legal advice on the best way of obtaining charitable status for itself.*

- *The department requires NAYPIC to provide an outline work programme for the paid staff following the AGM by 31 December. We would then expect a report on the first year's activities to be provided in September 1992. The release of each year's funding will depend on receiving a satisfactory report on the previous year's work. We should also like to meet NAYPIC representatives from time to time to discuss the progress of NAYPIC's work.*

- *Two copies of NAYPIC's accounts, audited to professional standards, are to be provided as soon as possible, but not later than six months after the end of your financial year.*

NAYPIC had not received any government funding for the past 19 months. It was the third time in their short history that funding had been discontinued, and although the London Office had continued to employ two workers (funded by the LBGU), much of NAYPIC's 'national' activities had, once again, to be sustained as best they could by the voluntary efforts of young people. The restoration of government funding provided an opportunity for NAYPIC to overcome past difficulties and re-establish itself.

As the extent of both political and professional pressure to restore the grant showed, NAYPIC was seen as an important organisation in terms of the government's growing commitment to the children's rights agenda. This included the introduction of complaints procedures and increased recognition of taking into account the child's '*wishes and feelings*' in the wake of the Children Act 1989. NAYPIC was seen as being able to contribute to the practice of local authorities in both these areas. Also, serious allegations of physical, sexual and emotional abuse in children's homes had come to light in Staffordshire and Leicestershire. And the UK was set to ratify the United Nations Convention on the Rights of the Child in 1991.

NAYPIC, the end

Despite the extent of the past difficulties there was a lot of good will towards NAYPIC succeeding. It had contributed significantly to the introduction of the new children's rights agenda, and it was to be hoped that it could now contribute to its implementation. However, it was not to be.

NAYPIC did succeed in maintaining a high level of casework, receiving calls from young people directly, as well as social workers, foster carers, and other professionals. In October 1991, its last report: *NAYPIC, The Time for Change* outlined the organisation's aims, activities and organisational structure.[79] But it never really recovered from its earlier divisions. They cast a long shadow. For those who had been involved in earlier struggles, the conflicts and internal divisions had left scars. The demise of the In Care Company with the loss of expertise from over 25 ex-care young people - many who had been involved in NAYPIC from the beginning, and the members of the professional advisory group, left a major gap in administrative and day-to-day support for new and inexperienced NAYPIC staff. There were long delays in submitting both work reports and accounts. The 1991-92 accounts were not submitted until June 1993 and the 1992-3 accounts were also overdue.

At a meeting on 23 September 1993 between representatives of NAYPIC and the Department of Health, NAYPIC was informed that its failure to provide audited accounts and work reports would result in immediate grant suspension.. The LBGU also decided to cease funding the London office from December 1993. By March 1994, NAYPIC's offices in Manchester and London were closed. For the first time since NAYPIC's inception in 1979 there was to be no national organisation to promote the voice of young people in care.

Chapter 12

A National Voice

'A new organisation for young people who are or have been in care is needed which should be supported from statutory as well as charitable sources.'

'Local authorities should make direct use of the experience of the children and young people they look after in developing policy, practice and training for services for children living away from home.'

(Recommendations from Sir William Utting's Report, *People Like Us*, 1997)

The demise of the National Association of Young People in Care pleased no one, even though its latter years had been very troubled ones. It posed the question, what was to be made of the government's commitment to promoting 'children's rights' when its funding for the only user organisation representing young people in care had been withdrawn? However, there was to be no sustained recriminations or resumption of hostilities between the different factions, but more a recognition of the difficulties faced by young people in care in running their own organisation, and a resignation to the attendant realities. A silent consensus about the need for space and reflection prevailed.

Testing the waters - a feasibility study

In August 1996, after a two year gap, the Department of Health commissioned First Key, an organisation who had experience of working with groups of young people leaving care, to carry out a one year feasibility study.[80] They were to report to the department on the role, structure, funding and management of a *'national mechanism representing children and young people in care.'* The timing of the commission was no coincidence.

The government's Review of Safeguards for Children Living Away from Home, chaired by Sir William Utting, had been set up in June that year, as a political response to the reported widespread abuses of children and young people in children's homes.[81] The review had specifically noted that many of the children who were abused were unable to tell anybody. But there was an irony. A feasibility study to determine the future of an organisation for young people in care was sparked by abuse scandals, yet such revelations when raised by *Who Cares?* in the 1970's and NAYPIC in the 1980's and London NAYPIC in 1990 failed to generate such political or professional concerns.

First Key's study was overseen by a development group of 13 young people. Its work was to include: focus groups with children and young people; a series of meetings - with 'adult organisations' representing young people, existing in-care organisations and key individuals; questionnaires distributed to local in-care and aftercare groups, children's rights officers and advocates, and children and young people in care. 'Regional debates' with interested groups were also planned.

The study was widely publicised to young people - 16,500 flyers were included in *Who Cares?* magazine which was circulated widely to young people in care, as well as articles in local in care newsletters. The study also aimed to explore the lessons to be learnt from NAYPIC's experiences, as well as other national in-care organisations, including the Australian Association of Young People in Care (AAYPIC), Voices of Young People in Care, Northern Ireland, and Who Cares? Scotland.

First Key reported to the Department of Health in October 1997. It concluded that it had found:

'overwhelming support for a national in-care organisation for children and young people who are, or have been looked after derived from a broad constituency of care experienced young people, existing local in-care groups, children's rights and advocacy projects, academics, statutory agencies and voluntary child care organisations.' [82]

On the basis of its findings, First Key recommended to the Department of Health:[83]

- A national in-care organisation for England should be set up supported by a 'host' adult organisation.

- The organisation receives a level of funding such that it is relatively secure and that enables it to develop regional initiatives and structures.

- The organisation gives priority to developing and maintaining close formal links with local in-care groups and should hold regional debates with local in-care groups on an annual basis.

- The structure should be representative of young people in foster as well as residential care, from all regions of the country, and there should not be separate organisations for young black people, disabled young people, and gay and lesbian young people.

- The constitution should ensure that young people have control over all matters associated with the policy and activities of the organisation, it should be membership based and open to all those with a care experience, irrespective of age.

- There should not be an age limit on those people employed by the organisation, although recruitment should reflect that this is a young person's organisation.

- A national executive should be established to manage the organisation consisting of care experienced young people, two thirds of whom should be nominated from local in-care and after care groups.

- An advisory group, made up from voluntary and statutory organisations and key individuals who have had a positive impact on the care system should be formed.

- Ongoing monitoring should take place during the first three years to ensure that the organisation is meeting its objectives..

The timing of First Key's feasibility study could not have been better. Sir William Utting's report, *People Like Us*, in response to the children's homes scandals, was presented to the new Labour Government in August 1997. Its recommendations included:[84]

'A new organisation for young people who are or have been in care is needed which should be supported from statutory as well as charitable sources.'

'Local authorities should make direct use of the experience of the children and young people they look after in developing policy, practice and training for services for children living away from home.'

The Department of Health received the recommendations of the First Key feasibility study in October 1997, just two months after Utting's report, and having also set up a Ministerial Task Force chaired by then Secretary of State, Frank Dobson, to respond to Utting's recommendations. The department accepted First Key's recommendations and invited them to act as the 'host organisation' and apply for money to set up a national in-care organisation.

In July 1998, First Key received a three year grant from the Department of Health to establish the organisation. The *Government's Response to the Children's Safeguard Review* was published in November 1998 and in it reported:

'The government has commissioned First Key to take forward a project to establish a group to provide a national voice for looked after children and those formerly in the care of local authorities and has agreed Section 64 funding of £450,000 over the next three years.' [85]

Funding *A National Voice* was seen as an important component of the new government's commitment to reform and modernise children's services. In September 1998 the *Quality Protects* programme was launched by the Department of Health. It provided substantial government funding linked to specific service objectives to produce better outcomes for children and young people who were looked after or in need.[86] Also in November 1998, the Department of Health's White Paper, *Modernising Social Services* was published, introducing an extensive set of reforms to improve the protection of children living away from home.[87] Young people's participation was central to the government's modernisation and safeguarding agenda.

Following the success of the funding application, the 'old steering group,' including the 13 young people that had led the First Key feasibility study, was re-formed and met regularly to carry out the detailed planning required to bring about the new organisation, building on the ground work already undertaken. This was reflected in the proposed structure of the organisation:

- A management committee – consisting of young people with direct experience of care, two thirds nominated by local in-care groups.

- An advisory group – including representatives from adult organisations and key individuals with significant contributions to make.

- A national co-ordinator – a young adult with direct experience of care.

- A national advisor – an advisory and mentoring role, care experience desirable.

- Five regional development workers – to be located in the North East, North West, Midland, South East, and South West.

- Five regional forums – of young people in care.

- Group and individual members.

A National Voice – a new beginning

The first National Co-ordinator was appointed in April 1999 and based in the new head office in Manchester. A National Voice was officially launched at the House of Commons, member's dining room, on 24 June 1999. John Hutton, then Undersecretary of State for Health, gave the organisation the government's official seal of approval.

Following its successful House of Commons launch, A National Voice (ANV) started work. It organised 'regional roadshows' during the summer of 1999. These were held in Bridlington, St Helens, Derbyshire, Hertfordshire and Gloucestershire, local authorities which had all sponsored the events. About 400 young people in care attended these fun roadshows which included everything from DJ 'mixing and scratching' workshops to aromatherapy and circus skills. But, as well as being a lot of fun, these events also provided an opportunity for young people in care to find out about A National Voice (ANV), and for ANV to seek young people's views about what they should be doing. There were also postcards for young people to fill in for ANV to contact them, as well as 'dear director' post cards.

Responding to 'Me, Survive, Out There?'

It was a busy summer. In August 1999 ANV organised a national conference attended by 109 young people, to explore their views about *Me, Survive, Out There?*, the government's consultative proposals to reform the law for young people leaving care.[88] It was in 1973, 25 years earlier, that the *Ad-Lib* group had first raised concerns about the plight of young people leaving care, and the torch had been passed on to *Who Cares?* and NAYPIC.

'budget limitations should not limit their choices and opportunities'

At the event young people were generally supportive of the proposals to strengthen the law in regard to planning, preparation and after care. ANV commented that the *'current system of support for care leavers is often patchy and inadequate and fails to prepare young people for independence or to offer meaningful ongoing support.'*[89] ANV's main recommendations included the need for more flexible support, *'in particular out of hours support and having drop-in centres and free-phone numbers.'* They also suggested that *'if (leaving care) does not work out, they should have a supportive home to return to.'*

They also wanted *'a system that conveys hope, ambition and confidence in them, budget limitations should not limit their choices and opportunities.'* This should include *'support to pursue further and higher education, or to establish themselves within a job*, and better, *'nationally consistent'* financial support to achieve these ends, *'not to be dependent on benefits.'* It would also include *'plans to promote the health, emotional and mental well being of young people as well as addressing practical needs.'*

They also argued that care leavers should be far more involved in leaving care services.

'Care experienced young people have a significant role to play. Care experience should be a 'desirable criterion' in the recruitment of workers. More care experienced people within the system could have the effect of changing negative attitudes to young people from care and help in engineering more trust between young people and the system.'[90]

A report based on the day was written up and sent to the government.[91] This was important in that it showed that ANV, like its predecessor NAYPIC, was prepared to influence government policy. ANV also made presentations at national conferences including those organised by the Department of Health on *Quality Protects*, Fostering Network, the Association of Children's Lawyers, as well as local events including a children's rights day in Essex.

ANV secures further funding

The first year's activities of A National Voice were concentrated on raising its profile among young people, local authorities and the government, in the different ways described above. This was achieved in the main by the efforts of only one full time member of staff and the voluntary efforts of young people on the management group. The next stage was to develop the regional structure - although the department's

'Plans to promote the health, emotional and mental well-being of young people'

grant only provided funding for two regional workers, one to be based in London and the other in the head office in Manchester. The first national co-ordinator, who played a key role in getting ANV going, left in August 2001. But a further three years Department of Health funding had been secured, from April 2001 to March 2004. This followed the submission of a detailed business plan which began:

'A National Voice exists as a care experienced, young person led organisation to make a positive change for children and young people in and leaving care.'[92]

The plan also stated:

'In the long term it is anticipated that A National Voice will become independent of First Key and be an independent voluntary agency with charitable status. In 2001 there was still a need for the management, guidance and supervision provided by First Key. A detailed plan and timescales for independence would be deferred for the foreseeable future.'[93]

An acting coordinator was appointed from August 2001, initially to work three days a week, and then full–time from October 2001. Regional development workers were appointed in the Manchester office, and in London. The high profile built up by ANV was maintained through their presentations at national events and by the day-to-day casework carried out by the national office in response to requests for advice from young people, social workers, carers, students, politicians, civil servants and other interested groups. By the end of 2001, ANV had entered the techno-communication age by setting up the website: www.anationalvoice. org. And in December 2001 the acting coordinator was appointed to the national coordinator post with immediate effect.

By the beginning of 2002, A National Voice had five full time workers, four based in Manchester (the national coordinator; a North West regional development worker; an administrator; and a young people's involvement worker), and one in London, (a Southern regional development worker). The organisation continued to raise its profile through participating in national and regional events, including the Department of Health's Quality Protects annual conference. It was also to become an active member of the Associate Parliamentary Group for Children and Young People In and Leaving Care. Politically, this group was highly influential – it's aim was to raise the awareness of Members of Parliament about the issues, policies and practices that influenced young people's lives in care.

Amplify 2002

A National Voice also planned *Amplify*, a major residential *'fun consultation event run by and for young people from care'* for the summer of 2002. Recruitment was slow until the then president of the ADSS heard about the event from the national coordinator and made it clear to his members they should support it.

On 17 and 18 August 2002, *Amplify* was held at Leicester University. It was fully endorsed by the government:

'The Department of Health gives its support to this important event. Participation underpins the Quality Protects programme and is a priority for the special grant. The department encourages councils to support their young people in taking part. We want ANV to hear the views and voices from young people across the country.'[94]

The *Amplify* event proved a great success. Some 150 young people, aged between 13 and 21, from all over England attended. The poet, Lemm Sissay, who had contributed to NAYPIC's *Black and In Care* conference in 1984 - nearly 20 years earlier - was the opening speaker! During Saturday, the first day of *Amplify*, a range of creative, informative and practical workshops were held. The following day, Sunday, was all about listening to the voices of young people on a range of issues, using a consultative process designed entirely by young people themselves. Following the event, a feedback report and video were planned. This involved a lot of hard work that was to occupy the efforts of the ANV team during the remainder of 2002.

The *Amplify* video and report were launched at a special meeting of the Associate Parliamentary Group for Children and Young People In and Leaving Care on 19 March 2003.[95] The event was sponsored by the Prince's Trust and included Members of Parliament and the House of Lords, the Department of Health, local councillors and representatives from statutory and voluntary child care organisations. Jacqui Smith, the then Minister of State at the Department of Health was unable to attend but her senior civil servant represented the department. ANV's Amplify report and video highlighted the main issues that had arisen from their consultation event with young people in care.[96]

Young people wanted more recognition of the impact of being *'moved from place to place'* and not being able to put down roots. Many of the young people who attended the *Amplify* event felt that their needs and wishes about accommodation were not being taken into consideration. Also, when they were moved, young people wanted to be *'given suitcases not black bin bags'* as was the practice in many local authorities.

Young people were also very angry that 'sleepovers' at their friends' homes were subject to police checks, especially when their school mates who were not in care didn't have to go through this process.

'There's too much bureaucracy, we need to stop police checks for little matters such as this. My mate Tom stays at his mate's house all the time, if he can why can't I? Am I being punished for being in care?'

Most of the young people who attended the *Amplify* event felt that they left care too young, before they were prepared or ready to leave.

'Local authorities should not put pressure, or quietly encourage young people to leave at 16, getting them off the books to free up places.'

Young people wanted a wider and better choice of accommodation, as well as good quality ongoing support after leaving care. They also wanted more information. In one of the consultation groups at the *Amplify* event, only a fifth of young people had heard about the Children (Leaving Care) Act 2000, which had been introduced in October 2001. Some young people said that they were very confused about leaving care grants and the money they were entitled to, especially the fact that young people from different areas were receiving different amounts. It was strongly suggested that *'the same amount nation-wide should be in place.'*

As regards their experience of care, young people at the *Amplify* event wanted to be more involved in their reviews and for their views to be taken more into account. They were also very concerned about the frequency of changes in social workers, key workers and aftercare workers, and the inconsistency and lack of trust arising from so much change - *'one month's notice is insufficient to end relationships properly.'* Racism in the care system was also spoken of, as was the lack of foster carers from minority ethnic backgrounds.

Finally, most of the young people who attended *Amplify* said they didn't know how to make a formal complaint, and were confused about the different roles of advocates, independent visitors and children's rights officers. But they overwhelmingly supported the view that they should have access to an independent person if they had concerns about their care – *'there should be an independent person who doesn't come from social services and isn't a carer or foster parent.'*

Following ANV's Amplify presentation at the meeting of the Associate Parliamentary Group, a senior civil servant representing the Department of Health, responded that the government '*would be pleased to have further discussions*' with ANV on how these issues might be addressed. But that was not the end of proceedings. At the same parliamentary meeting, A National Voice also launched the foster care campaign, based upon the views of young people. It was focussed on: '*Hellos*' – to improve the experience of young people going into care through pre-placement visits, better information and clearer expectations; '*Involvement*' – to improve young people's access to services including the use of advocacy services, in-care groups, and information; and '*Goodbyes*' – to improve the situation around young people leaving placements and those experiencing placement changes.[97]

The *Amplify* report and video presented at the House of Commons in March 2003, the launch of the foster care campaign and the *Amplify* event in summer 2003, were key landmarks in establishing A National Voice as a credible organisation for young people in care. It had also shown through its day-to-day activities that it was a viable organisation with a strong administrative foundation to cope with future activities.

A National Voice under threat

But in June 2003 this new found strength and optimism, and indeed the future of A National Voice itself, was under threat by the closure of its host organisation, First Key. Following a sustained period of severe financial difficulties, First Key was deemed by its trustees to be no longer a viable organisation, and it ceased work on 4 June 2003. As First Key was the fund holder for ANV this also meant that 'legally' ANV faced closure and its staff faced redundancy on the same date. This duly happened on 4 June 2003. But not all was lost – a lot was happening behind the scenes. First, the national coordinator had involved Hilton Dawson MP (an adviser to ANV) and he highlighted the current situation facing ANV to the then Children's Minister, Margaret Hodge. Second, there was an emergency meeting of the Associate Parliamentary Group, at which the national coordinator captured the moment, saying: '*A National Voice needs an emergency foster placement to host us*'. Third, when the extent of First Key's financial difficulties had first emerged, including the threat to ANV, discussions had been held with potential new 'host' organisations. In response, the Prince's Trust, although not in a position to employ ANV staff, agreed to provide some financial support, whilst further discussions took place.

The political pressure paid off. On 24 June 2003, the Department of Health, shaken by the possibility of the demise of A National Voice, also issued a paper aimed at recruiting potential 'host organisations' including the 'carrot' - payment of core funding to the new 'host' until 31 March 2004, the end of the grant period.[98] However, unexpectedly, given the department's strong support for their work, the proposals also seemed to cast a shadow over the longer term future of ANV, from April 2004.

'Since the idea of ANV was proposed, there has been important developments in the way children and young people participate in their care and in wider development of care services. Many of these have been inspired and funded by the Quality Protects Programme, which comes to an end as a separately funded initiative by April 2004.'

- *Most, if not every local authority, has its own looked after children group.*
- *Some groups of care experienced young people now meet on a regional basis.*
- *Virtual technology such as CareZone creates new opportunities for involving larger groups of care experienced young people.*
- *The importance of listening to younger children and those in foster care has been recognised.*
- *There is greater understanding of the range of needs of looked after young people – participation work must respond to looked after young people from across every background and reach out to significant groups of young people in care such as children with learning difficulties in residential schools.*

As QP is ending and the services it supported will now have to be included in the routine work of social services, and given all the developments in children's participation activity, now is a good time to review the work of young people's groups. The Children and Families Directorate of DfES will be arranging for this over the coming months.

One of the issues that it will need to tackle is how the voice of children and young people in care and care leavers can be represented from April 2004. It will be very important that ANV contributes to this review and takes part in plans to ensure that the voice of children and young people in care and care leavers is heard and that services respond to what they say.' [99]

Following the circulation of the department's letter, the national coordinator, working in a voluntary capacity since June 2003, and the management committee of ANV, formally approached the Prince's Trust to ask if they would be their 'host organisation' for the remaining period of the grant. This arrangement was accepted by the department.

A National Voice's re-launch

A National Voice was re-launched in London in October 2003 as ANV *re-loaded* - promoting a second edition of the *Amplify* report with additional recommendations for improving the care system, as well as outlining their foster care campaign and information about their new website. The re-launch received good publicity. Under the headline '***Bin the bureaucracy***' the Guardian picked up on some of the key issues of the *Amplify* report:

'The practice of bundling possessions into bin liners when moving placements is one of the most hated aspects of life for young people in care. That and an end to the infuriating red tape that prevents young people in care from having a 'sleepover' at a friend's house before weeks of checks by the authorities beforehand, are among the key recommendations published this week by A National Voice.' [100]

(The Guardian 15 March 2003)

The Guardian report cited A National Voice committee member.

'Things like the bin bags are the small things that do the damage, the stuff that really gets up people's noses. It's partly the lack of dignity, partly the symbolism: bin bags are for carrying rubbish.' [101]

However, despite the success of ANV's re-launch, the shadow of the government's pending review of '*the work of young people's groups*' hung over them. This was to be carried out between September and December 2003. The department commissioned a team of three - two researchers and a young person, to carry out the review. Following meetings with the management committee of A National Voice and other key organisations, a framework of topics for the review was agreed and a list of individuals, organisations and people to contact was drawn up. Questionnaires, face-to face interviews, telephone interviews and group discussions were carried out to explore people's views. The review was published in December 2003. It came to very similar conclusions as the feasibility study undertaken before ANV was established:

'There is clearly both a strong case and a great deal of support for a national organisation of young people in care amongst young people and adults. In the light of this we strongly urge the department to take a clear and determined stand on the future of the national organisation. By this we mean that if the National

Organisation of Young People in Care has a hope of being a secure, robust, functioning and young people led organisation, which truly represents the voices of young people in care, it has to be powerfully backed and properly financed. If it is not, it will be immediately limited in how successful it can be for young people or for the care system.

This organisation needs everyone involved with it (government, local authorities, mentors and supporting organisations, staff and young people) to sign up to its values and principles and to support it in a realistic and identifiable way. It needs central government to endorse it, to direct local authorities to promote it, to listen to it and to fund it adequately. To do anything less would be to pay lip-service to young people's abilities, commitment and determination and therefore actively detrimental to the young people who put their trust and ambition in it. The message from all over is 'do it properly or not at all!' [102]

On 26 February 2004, the department accepted the recommendations of the group and announced its support for the continuation of A National Voice, supported by 'host organisation' the Prince's Trust:

'This decision has been reached after consultation with our Minister. We would hope that the Prince's Trust will provide the support to ANV to enable it to progress to becoming a more independent organisation over the next five years.' [103]

The lifting of the threat to A National Voice's future meant that it could, at least for the time being, get on with its work, with some commitment to the future. In fact, since the re-launch in October 2003 work had been gathering pace.

Campaigning activities

The new edition of the *Amplify* report and its recommendations provided a strong platform for campaigning on a number of fronts.

First, the campaign to end '*bin bagging*' – the practice of moving young people's possessions in a rubbish bag when they changed placements or moved out of care – was widely promoted. A label '*THIS IS NOT A SUITCASE CAMPAIGN*', attached to black bin bags was distributed to all local authorities. A second label, also attached to the folded bin bag, read:

'This is NOT a suitcase and yet many children and young people in care are moved to and from care placements with their possessions in BIN BAGS. This is one of the things about the care system in England we want to change.'

A *No Bin Bag Charter* was also launched for organisations to sign up to, and the campaign has also been promoted through the All Party Parliamentary Group for Children In and Leaving Care at the House of Commons and at various conferences. The then Minister, Margaret Hodge was given a bin bag by a young person in Parliament, and after their annual conference the Liberal Democrats contacted ANV, saying that they had signed up to the campaign.

The campaign included the *Refuse Collection Fashion Shows* held in Manchester and Belfast during 2004. Events were also held in London in 2005 and 2006 – including an event at Tate Britain (see below) chaired by Lord Laming with hip hop music and all! The catwalk protest included young people from care modelling outfits made out of bin bags, as well as a DVD of the show. Following the Belfast show 150 independent fostering providers, hosted by Fostering Network, got together to adopt a *No Bin Bag* policy and arrange for the DVD to be used as part of their training packs.

The campaign continues today – currently 80 per cent of local authorities have signed up.

Second, and also arising from the *Amplify* report, ANV has campaigned for making '*sleepovers*' at friend's houses simpler for young people living in care. This has led directly to new departmental guidance being issued to local authorities to improve this situation.

Third, ANV is campaigning for a national minimum leaving care grant, to ensure all young people setting up home for the very first time receive the same amount wherever they may live. They want to end the 'postcode lottery' approach - as many young people are upset to find out that people living in a neighbouring authority are getting lots more money to start their independent life.

Fourth, in October 2004 ANV launched their accommodation campaign. This was based on a survey of just under 600 respondents, 300 care leavers, aged 16 to 25, and 300 professionals who work with them. The report, *There's No Place Like Home* was published in December 2005.[104]

Their survey found that just over half of young people felt that they had no real choice in the accommodation offered to them; just under a third did not feel safe in their accommodation and that their accommodation did not meet their needs; half of the young people surveyed thought that housing departments were not aware of the particular needs and circumstances of young care leavers; and 12 per cent

Barnardo's, Tate Britain, The Social Care Institute for Excellence and A National Voice
invite you to a reception on
27th October at 6.30pm at Tate Britain
to mark the 5th Anniversary of the Children (Leaving Care) Act 2000.

*The reception will also celebrate A National Voice's 'This Is **Not** A Suitcase' campaign and include the 'Refuse Collection Bin Bag Fashion Show'*

Please rsvp to Michael Phillips
Tel: 0151-488-1119
Email: michael.phillips@barnardos.org.uk

'The latest ploy has been the Bin Bag Fashion Show'

of young people were living in bed and breakfast or hostel accommodation and a similar percentage were staying with friends.

Just over three quarters of the leaving care workers and personal advisors surveyed thought that young people were still leaving care at too young an age and with inadequate preparation. Most workers also thought that insufficient attention was paid to emotional support, and that poverty restricted their social networks as well as access to participate in other activities. The great majority of workers surveyed thought that lack of support for young people contributed to them being evicted from their accommodation. Finally, most housing workers recognised that care leavers found it difficult to manage their rent and finances. But over half had not received any training or information on the needs of young care leavers.

The main aims of *There's No Place Like Home* campaign are for care leavers to be 'well prepared' for adult life; have a 'good choice' of accommodation; that is 'safe' and 'well supported'; and that is 'affordable', 'comfortable' and 'secure'.

Fifth, in October 2005 ANV launched its *'Please Sir, Can I have some more? Education Campaign Survey.*[105] This was based upon a consultation exercise with young people in care who told ANV that their number one issue was 'getting an education and qualifications'. The consultation process also identified what they saw as the barriers to getting an education whilst living in care:

'not having enough say in education choices' 'having unsuitable accommodation' 'moving around too much' 'having different carers' 'not believing in myself – others not believing in me' 'not enough financial support, for books, living costs, fees' 'not enough support from carers, social workers or personal advisors' 'feeling different and being labelled at school'

'a quiet place to study' 'no help with homework and study' 'bullying' 'not enough careers advice' 'feeling as though you have missed out on too much education to go back' 'not enough training given to those who look after you to assist in your education' 'the emotional and psychological effects of your personal life' 'not enough support from schools or teachers.'[106]

As well as campaigning, A National Voice has continued to contribute to national policy networks and governmental consultative processes, '*ensuring the voices of our members are heard and included in government level decision making.*' It has also maintained a high public profile. It was involved in the planning of the BBC 'Taking Care' series during two weeks in February 2004. This led to several national and local TV and radio interviews by its members talking about their experiences of life in care. In September 2009, it was also involved in the Channel 4 series about the lives of young people living in and leaving care.

The website has also proved very popular: in one month alone it received over 5,000 hits. The site includes prose and poetry from young people. Many of the topics and their words echo the voices of the *Ad-Lib* and *Who Cares?* young people nearly 30 years earlier, especially their experience of movement and disruption, and the loss of family:

'I've been in care five times since I was six years old. I had my seventh birthday in care then a few months afterwards I went back. That happened another four times. When I was nine I came for the fifth time, then the court said I had to stay in till I am eighteen.'

Rachel (age 12)

You Didn't

When I gained good grades
You didn't celebrate

When I was happy
You didn't smile

When I was sad
You didn't cry
When I was upset
You didn't ask why

When I was sick
You didn't care
When I needed you the most
You weren't there

You are so far away
You are so far away

You are so far away

Marchu (aged 16)

But it is not all doom and gloom!

Because I'm in Care

I'm trouble don't you know
But I have no criminal record

I'm thick don't you know
With four GCSEs and a diploma in social care

It's my fault don't you know
But I never asked that social worker to land on my door

I'm worthless don't you know
But I have a three year modelling contract

I should not have a place in society
But I am loved and cared for greatly

I will live off the dole for the rest of my life
Highly unlikely, I'm going to Uni. In September

I ask for society to open its eyes
And realise we are stereotyped into a disguise

I have proved by my achievements so far
That I can shine brightly
Just like a star

(Louise, aged 18)

A National Voice – moving on: 2006-2011

In May 2006, A National Voice became an independent organisation and moved from its 'host organisation' the Princess Trust, to its own London offices. For the first time in the history of the rights movement, an organisation existed that not only represented and campaigned for young people in care, but also controlled its own administration and funding. It owed a big debt to the struggles of *Ad-Lib, Who Cares?*, and most of all to NAYPIC. But now it could move on.

Care Matters

During 2006 and 2007, ANV was involved in the Care Matters consultation process which resulted in the White Paper *Care Matters; Time for Change* and the implementation plan *Care Matters: Time to deliver for children in care*. This included a meeting with then Prime Minister, Tony Blair, at which the national coordinator stole the show with her response to his question about 'what is most important for young people in care?' *'stability, stability, stability'* – was the immediate response (echoing Blair's well-known *education, education, education quote)!* ANV's evidence *'These Matter To Us'* suggested the following changes young people want to the care system[107]:

- To have more information and more choice about what happens.
- To have stability in both care and school places.
- To have more support to stay in touch with people who are important to them.
- To stay in care longer and not have to move to independent living until they are ready.
- To have safe and decent accommodation when they leave care.
- To have the chance to meet and share experiences with others from care.
- To be able to make mistakes and still get support as young adults.
- To have their voices listened to and their views and opinions take into account.

They conclude their evidence: '*Really, it's nothing more than anyone would provide for their own child – which is what we want. Politicians, councillors, local authorities and child care staff should always ask themselves, 'would this be good enough for my child?' – if it isn't then it isn't good enough for children in care. This is what we want from Care Matters and we believe that A National Voice can help in ensuring positive changes come about after the consultation*'.

The Lilac project

In June 2007, A National Voice launched its Lilac project (Leading Improvements for Looked After Children) at the House of Commons. Initially, this trained young people who have spent a lot of their lives in care, to become inspectors of children's services. The initiative was a result of pilot projects held in York and West Sussex which confirmed that children and young people in care find it a lot easier to talk to young people who have similar experiences to themselves. In their inspection role, care experienced young people have been looking at how well local authorities involve children and young people in their own care, in the planning and evaluation of the services which shape their lives, and how effectively they deal with complaints. The importance of this work was highlighted by the government in the report *Care Matters: Time to deliver for children in care.*

Currently LILAC has expanded its role with local authorities by training care experienced young people to carry out assessments of how well services involve and consult with children and young people, and to deliver training on participation. The latter is linked to seven standards developed by care experienced young people, reflecting what is important to them, including: shared values; style of leadership; structures; staff; recruitment and selection; care planning and review, and complaints and advocacy

ANV gives evidence to the House of Commons, Children, Schools and Families Committee on Looked after Children

Following in the footsteps of NAYPIC, who gave evidence to the parliamentary Select Committee on Children in Care in 1983, A National Voice did likewise in 2008, 25 years later. In March 2008, the chief executive (previously, the national coordinator) appeared as an expert witness before the Committee and gave evidence of how young people experienced the care system, and what changes would make their lives better. The report of the Committee, published in April 2009, showed that ANV's evidence proved to be highly influential in respect of many of their recommendations[108].

ANV stressed the importance of young people having time to develop a relationship with their social workers, especially when they have large case loads. Committee recommendation 7 read:

- *'We recommend that the government consider...the practicalities and possible benefits of guidance specifying optimum caseloads for social workers.'*

Concerns were also voiced about social work practices adding another layer for young people. Recommendation ten included

- *'The views of children and young people are given particular prominence in the evaluation of the (social work practice) pilots.'*

ANV's chief executive's evidence drew attention to the contribution of residential care for young people who cannot live with their own family, or who have had repeated placement breakdowns in foster care. Recommendation 24 included:

- *'The government commissions research on the flexible use of residential care as part of a planned package of care.'*

The large variations in the way young people experience living in care in different areas of the country was also highlighted in ANV's evidence - *there are almost '150 care systems' in 150 local authorities.* This was also taken up by the Committee in recommendation 30 of the report:

- *'The quality of experience that children have in care seems to be governed by luck to an utterly unacceptable degree...we urge the government to place the highest priority on ensuring that every child gets everything they are entitled to.'*

It was also made clear to the Committee of the need for Children in Care Councils and Pledges to have 'real teeth.' Recommendation 37 read:

- *'The government must spell out how local authorities will be held accountable for robust development of their Children in Care Councils and Pledges, and the impact these measures have on improving practice. It is not clear at present what the consequences will be for a corporate parent that fails to keep its promise to children, nor what action a child will be able to take if those promises are broken. Pledges must be detailed enough to be meaningful to young people, and we urge the government to encourage local authorities to show ambition in their undertakings.'*

ANV's evidence stressed the importance of young people having independent representation of their views. This was recognised in Recommendations 39 and 40:

- *'Advocacy services should be routinely available for all looked-after children whenever decisions about their care are being made, not just when they wish to make a complaint.'*

- *'The duty on local authorities to ascertain and give consideration to children's views when decisions about their care are made should be strengthened by a requirement for independent reviewing officers to record those views when care plans are reviewed.'*

ANV drew attention to the delays experienced by young people in accessing the child and adolescent mental health services. Recommendation 44 included:

- *'Children and young people should have guaranteed access to child and adolescent mental health services.'*

ANV's view that young people's experiences of leaving care could be improved by young people leaving care later, and receiving better personal and housing support, was included in recommendations 46, 49 and 54:

- *'The government should show more ambition by making a commitment to narrowing the gap between the average age of leaving care and the age of independence for other young people. Remaining in care in some form until at least 21 should become the norm.'*

- *'Young people who find they are not yet ready for independence are able, and encouraged, to revert to a higher level of support.'*

- *'We seek reassurance from the government that funding will be made available to local authorities that experience particular difficulties in*

finding suitable accommodation for care leavers due to housing shortages.
We recommend that the government extends the new 'sufficient placements'
duty to include supported and independent accommodation for those
leaving care.'

ANV drew attention to the dangers of young people being vulnerable to sexual exploitation on leaving care. Recommendation 50 included:

- *'We urge the government to analyse ways in which features of the care*
  system itself expose young people to greater danger (of sexual exploitation),
  and take urgent steps to protect care leavers from this sort of exploitation.'

Finally, the importance of young people's views in undertaking the annual stock take of the care system was stressed by ANV to the Committee. Recommendation 69 included:

- *'We recommend that children's views and their satisfaction with the care*
  system should form a crucial part of the evidence used in the stock take.'

In addition, twelve young people and ANV staff talked about their experiences of care and education, and how this could be improved. It proved to be a very positive experience for young people:

'It was great, I really enjoyed it and I think they really took our views on board.'

'The MP's really listened to and cared about what we had to say.'

It is clear that like NAYPIC, ANV succeeded in getting their view across – as is reflected in the published report of the Children, Schools and Families Committee.

The chief executive was also appointed to the Social Work Task Force and ANV is represented on the Social Work Reform Board.

Children in Care Councils and Pledges

In March 2008, ANV organised national events in London and Manchester called '*Get Your ACT 2gether*'. These brought together young people and front line workers to share their experiences of Children in Care Councils and 'Pledges' (or commitments by local authorities to services for young people in care) – both ways of increasing the participation of young people in the care system. Young people who had been members of the councils made presentations at these events.

The success of these events led to two further initiatives. First, ANV and the children's rights director for England organising regional meetings for Children in Care council chairs during 2010-2011 to share experiences about what works well, and; second, ANV mapping Children in Care Councils nationally - to ensure every local authority sets up a council and introduces their 'Pledge'. ANV also offered to assist them with this process.

Emotional wellbeing

In 2010, ANV published a report on the emotional wellbeing of 106 young people living in and leaving care[109]. Based on the views of young people, this highlighted the high levels of need – just over 80 per cent said they found 'everyday life difficult to cope with', and just under three quarters of the young people said that their emotional problems had affected their home life, relationships, education, work or leisure activities. The survey also showed that young people found it difficult approaching mental health professionals for help – but they did feel they could talk to 'friends', 'family', or a 'social worker or aftercare worker'. Their main recommendations included education to reduce the stigma attached to mental health services; helping young people develop emotional intelligence; more opportunities for young people to receive emotional support, including at the time of transition from care, and through peer support.

And finally, supersonic and bin bags!

To encourage young people in care to have role models, A National Voice has set up a supersonic website with personal profiles of ex-care adults who have got on very well in life. This includes a film about their lives in care, the barriers they have faced, and how they have overcome them. ANV has also continued its 'bin bag' campaign. By 2010, it had succeeded in persuading two thirds of local authorities in England to sign the 'no bin bag charter' showing their commitment to abolish this appalling practice. So they decided to make 2010 the year England goes 'bin bag free'!

Chapter 13

From Order Books to Bin Bags

This story began in the early 1970's with young people living in children's homes in Leeds campaigning to '*ban the book*'. Instead of clothing vouchers only to be used under strict staff supervision at one or two 'discount' shops, the Leeds *Ad-lib* group, the first of its kind in England, wanted young people in care to be given money to buy their clothes. They wanted the same choice of what to wear as other young people.

Thirty years later, A National Voice, the organisation representing young people in care in England, is campaigning to '*bin the bag*'. They want young people to be given suitcases not bin bags when they have to move their belongings. '*Bin bags are for carrying rubbish*' they point out. What does that say about how young people in care are seen today?

This book has told the story of the intervening years. It describes how the rights movement of young people in care came about. But it is also a commentary on the care experienced by the young people who during these years belonged to the Leeds *Ad-Lib* group, *Who Cares?*, the National Association of Young People In Care, Black and In Care, and A National Voice. It is *their* history of care. In completing this account, both the story of their movement, and their experiences of care, demand further reflection, not least to see if there are lessons to be learnt for the future.

The rights movement of young people in care

Building on the small beginnings of Leeds *Ad-Lib*, and the wider geographical foundations of *Who Cares?*, NAYPIC changed everything. It was their activities, including their local and national campaigns, their surveys, and their evidence to parliament that led to the views of young people in care being recognised in law, policy and practice. Key changes introduced by the Children Act 1989 owe a lot to their campaigns. This included complaints procedures, strengthening the law to assist young people leaving care, the recognition of 'racial origin, culture and language' - through the powerful contribution of Black and In Care, as well as other groups identified in Chapter 7 - and consolidating the consultative rights of young people in care. The latter provision, taking into account the *wishes and feelings* of young people, had a longer legal history but, as demonstrated during the 1980's, NAYPIC made it their own through their surveys of young people's views and the policies derived from them. By 1984, the House of Commons Committee report on Children In Care, which laid the foundations of the Children Act 1989, drew widely on NAYPIC's evidence *Sharing Care* and reported *'NAYPIC's growth has given children a voice of their own.'*[110]

But it was not just in influencing government policy that young people's 'wishes and feelings' mattered. They mattered at the local level, in the in-care groups, like Leeds *Ad-Lib*, that both supported young people during their care experience and campaigned to bring about changes in local policies and practices. Many local authorities introduced changes as a result of local group activity, often working with NAYPIC groups to change attitudes, train staff and improve local practices. By joining a local group and talking to others about their lives in care, young people discovered - often for the first time - that they were not alone. It also gave them the opportunity to get their views over to social services staff and 'outsiders', as well as try to bring about change. For many young people the 'rights movement' meant belonging to *my* group. It was in *my* group that they made new friends and grew in confidence.

But what is also remarkable is that during these 30 years it was left to some of the most vulnerable young people in society, young people in care, to challenge policies and practices that stigmatised and degraded them. After all, this was a period which saw the dawn of the new professional era of social work and the growing influence of the new welfare thinking, particularly upon child care law, policy and practice. It was also the period which witnessed the creation and expansion of social service departments that embraced the corporate managerial revolution in local government.

What this clearly shows is the ongoing need for a young person's organisation. It cannot be left solely to others to act *'in the child's best interests'* or be responsible for *'the child's welfare.'* However well trained the child care professional, or whatever the expertise of the manager, there remains the critical distinction between experiencing injustice and, to use professional jargon, 'empathising' with it. The former, in this context, defines the rights movement for young people in care, the latter merely professional concern. The former, through the involvement of young people in its groups and campaigns, turns the stigma from the young person back onto the system that is responsible for creating it. No social worker would wear a black bin bag to a management meeting to make a point!

From its early days, the rights movement for young people in care has also faced struggles over funding. The unexpected ending of the *Who Cares?* project in 1978 left young people feeling let down and 'used' in the interests of a professionally led project. But their anger was channelled into creating NAYPIC in 1979. Its activities were sustained by the voluntary efforts of members until 1983 when it secured its first government grant. However, despite the success of the work, the grant was not renewed until after a six month gap, resulting in three full-time workers, all ex-care young people, being laid off. NAYPIC secured a further two year grant, from April 1988 to March 1990 but this was suspended in January 1989, again resulting in young people being laid off. The grant was re-instated from August 1989, after a seven month gap, until March 1990. But NAYPIC's application for three year funding from March 1990 was initially rejected. They eventually received three year funding from October 1991, following a nineteen month gap. But even NAYPIC's successor, A National Voice, has had to cope with a four month funding gap, from June to October 2003, the national co-ordinator working without pay during this period.

As detailed in this account there were many reasons for the withdrawal of funding. NAYPIC's failure to be awarded charitable status cast a long shadow, particularly in being able to operate as a single organisation responsible for administering its own funding, as well as its work activities. Also, as outlined in this narrative, the complex organisational arrangements contributed to internal divisions and disputes, although it was not the only cause.

However, on reflection, it does seem that the withholding of funding on these occasions has been a very harsh measure given that it was a movement representing young people from care, and employing young people who had themselves been in care. Not what you would expect of a good parent. During these enforced periods of unemployment it was their commitment to the cause that kept the organisation going. Funding remains a difficult issue. Ideally, it should be independent of government and local authorities for young people to be able to campaign freely for changes in national and local policies. But, in reality, there are few other sources of funding. What these young people have demonstrated over these years is that they can, but at no little cost to themselves, survive funding crises. A National Voice is up and running and has succeeded in achieving independent status, responsible for its own finances. But it is still very dependent on government funding.

Looking back, this is a story of both individual and collective resilience – as distinct from a collection of misery memoirs. The young people who made the rights movement not only coped with many personal disadvantages derived from their family background and their experiences of care, but they worked together to improve the lives of other young people in care, even when faced - at times - with cuts in their own funding, professional indifference and managerial antagonism. It is also a story of altruism, borne out of their common suffering, as well as an anger to challenge the injustices they experienced. But, as may be forgotten, it is also a story of young people. The belief, the commitment, the impulse, the conflicts, the humour, the creativity; all owe a lot to youth. As one of the leaders of the 1976 Soweto school demonstration reflected 30 years on: 'The value of youth is they act on impulses, if we had thought about it we wouldn't have done it.' (Soweto Uprising, BBC2, 14/6/2008)

A young person's history of care

The young people who participated in the rights movement during these years also have a story to tell about the care they received.

For the young people who participated in the Leeds *Ad-Lib* group in the mid-1970's it was a care in part still touched by the long shadows of the poor law and charity. The administrative 'special arrangements' for school dinners and purchasing clothes were highly insensitive to the needs of young people in care and were experienced by them as stigmatising and controlling. This was reinforced by their lack of involvement in decisions that shaped their lives – what was happening to them when they were taken into care, and their lives in care, including their reviews and access to their personal files. It was also a care that was still desperately trying to recreate the idea of 'the family' in children's homes whilst at the same time being subject to the authority of the bureaucratic parent.

The views of young people who participated in *Who Cares?* between 1975 and 1979 validated and extended many of the main themes identified by the *Ad-Lib* group concerning the identity of care during these years. Many of these young people experienced their 'care' as disruptive and controlling, excluding them from major decisions that affected them. It was a care that often failed to compensate young people for the problems they had come into care with, and some young people were to suffer further abuse at the hands of their 'carers'. Neither was there much public awareness of their plight.

NAYPIC's evidence to the 1983 House of Commons Socials Services Committee on Children in Care, *Sharing Care*, showed, from a young person's perspective, the very poor state of state care at the beginning of the 1980's. Their voices echoed many of the concerns raised during the previous decade, initially by Leeds *Ad-Lib* and later by Who Cares? The State didn't care enough about its most vulnerable children and young people to ensure that they were *all* provided with the quality of care to help them overcome the problems they had entered care with, and maximise their opportunities. As a consequence, many were condemned to a life of control, misery or indifference, including for some young people, further abuse by their 'carers'. In that sense their 'care' owed more to its poor law roots, than the new professional social work thinking. It was left to young people in care, through their own organisation, NAYPIC, in their evidence to the House of Commons Social Services Committee to show how their future might be made better than their past.

Between 1983 and 1985, the Black and In Care group gave a voice to black and minority ethnic young people. This revealed a 'white care' and a 'white life' that failed to recognise many of their needs at that time including: the neglect of culture and identity; ignorance about diet, health, hair and skin care; the lack of black and minority ethnic foster carers and staff in children's homes; racism within care; a failure to recognise the identity issues for young people of mixed parentage, and; the separation from family and community.

NAYPIC's 1986 evidence to the Wagner Group's *Review of Residential Care* also showed the overall poor state of care experienced by many young people – echoing the main findings in their 1983 evidence to the Social Services Committee, *Sharing Care*. They expressed particular concerns about the lack of opportunities for young people to participate in decisions which shaped their lives. This included criticism of the large number of authorities which still operated bulk buying for food, clothes and toiletries and other day-to-day requirements – even though these concerns had first been raised in 1973!

As detailed above, in the discussion of the 'rights movement of young people in care', the Children Act 1989 represented a watershed in respect of the rights of young people in care – and one which owed a lot to the contribution of NAYPIC. But a lot remained to be done in improving the quality of care.

A National Voice's 2002 *Amplify* conference, attended by 150 young people, also echoed earlier concerns about care, some dating back to the 1970's: being moved too much; feeling stigmatised by the 'special arrangements' for sleepovers at friends homes; being expected to leave care at 16 'to free-up places' for younger children; wanting to be more involved in their reviews; having too many changes of care staff and social workers; not knowing how to complain; and, finally, being given black bin bags' to move their belongings.

From 'order books' in 1975 to 'bin bags' in 2011, might suggest little had changed in 35 years. But this would be a too simplified account. Young people in care are far more likely to be fostered or live in smaller children's homes than 35 years ago. Also, as has been discussed earlier, there have been major changes in law, policy and practice to safeguard young people, consult with them and involve them in decision making - some of these changes directly influenced by the rights movement of young people in care.

But this is not to suggest a 30 year period of linear progression. Young people attending A National Voice's *Amplify* event, in the summer of 2002, echoed some of the main concerns raised by *Who Cares?* in 1977 and at NAYPIC's *Life in Care* conference in 1981. There are recurring themes during these years that have proved resistant to changes in organisational structures, national and local government policies and practices, as well as the 'latest' swings and fashions in child welfare ideas.

First, there is the 'loss' of family, not in the sense that many young people were orphaned or denied contact with their families but more in the feeling of being failed and betrayed by those who are expected to care for you. Over 30 years separate these verses from young people:

Unloved is to miss the love
that all parents should give
Yet they cast you aside
Put you out of their minds
They put you in care
There is no love there

(Young person, Leeds *Ad-Lib* Mag 1973)

When I was sick
You didn't care
When I needed you most
You weren't there

You were so far away
You were so far away
You were so far away
(Young person, A National Voice, 2005)

It is a depth of feeling that many young people are unable to come to terms with whist they are in the care of the 'bureaucratic parent'. And it is a feeling often reinforced by the ubiquity of 'the family' in school and work, as well as in pervading ideas and popular culture. There are no easy answers - some of the emotional scars may be lifelong. But adults who have been in care have spoken of the need for counselling and skilled help to help them put together the fragments of their lives: a coherent story will help them to move on.

Second, over these years, too many young people have spoken of their disrupted lives in care and the attendant painful consequences: moving between children's homes, foster care, their families, returning to care – for some young people on more than ten occasions whilst they were in care. Twenty-five years separate these young people's views:

'It's the coming and going that hurts. The first time you move to another place it hurts bad, so you build up a shell but one day the shell cracks.' (1977, Who Cares?[111])

'I wish they didn't move me all the time, I can't settle down anywhere.' (2002, Amplify[112])

The most fundamental requirement from care for these young people was for stability in their lives. Stability is the foundation stone of good quality care. It can provide the young person with a warm and redeeming relationship, or an attachment to a carer to compensate them for their disrupted family lives and their earlier problems. It can also provide often much-needed continuity in young people's lives, especially for those young people who enter care later, in their teenage years.

Young people who experience stable placements providing good quality care are more likely to feel better about themselves, succeed educationally and in their careers, settle after leaving care and achieve satisfactory integration in adulthood than young people who have experienced further movement and disruption during their time in care. A failure to provide young people with stability questions the fundamental rationale of the care system.

A third recurring theme is that many of these young people have thought at the time, or more often on reflection, that they left care to live independently too young. Again, 25 years separate these views.

'If you live with parents you're able to have a choice whether you leave home or not. But in care you get kicked out on your heels.' (1977, Who Cares?[113])

'You should be able to leave care when you are ready.' (2002 Amplify[114]*)*

Most of the young people whose voices were heard during these years left care before their 18th birthday. They were having to cope with the challenges and responsibilities of major changes in their lives at a far younger age than young people leaving the family home, often in their mid-to-late 20's: leaving foster care or their children's home and setting-up home; leaving school and going to college; leaving school and entering the world of work, or more likely, being unemployed and surviving on benefits; leaving care and becoming young parents. Their journey to adulthood was shorter, steeper and more hazardous than for most of their peers. They were denied the opportunity and space to deal with issues over time which is how most young people cope psychologically during this journey. The failure, to provide young people leaving care with a more gradual transition, more akin to other young people, also questions the rationale of the care system.

Fourth, the activities of the rights movement, from Who Cares? to a National Voice, has consistently exposed the wide variation in local authority practices and the quality of services young people receive. During these years, the national events - conferences, workshops, AGM's - gave young people the opportunity to talk about and to compare their experiences. This anecdotal evidence, was powerful, especially when published, as in *Who Cares? Young People in Care Speak Out, Life in Care*, Black and In Care and *Amplify*. But it was given more sustainable force by NAYPIC's, and subsequently, ANV's surveys of policy and practice. As this story has unfolded this has included evidence of wide variation in young people's participation in reviews, access to files, provision of guidebooks, 'control' of sanitary protection, preparation and support for leaving care, accommodation, and education. In these ways, the rights movement has been able to highlight the comparative or territorial injustices experienced by young people.

Punishment and abuse in care[115]

As long ago as 1977, young people in this narrative spoke and wrote about the '*hitting business*', the violence, discipline and physical punishment that was seen by some as a 'natural' part of their lives in children's homes. The ill-treatment that many suffered at the hands of their parents was, paradoxically, continued by their 'carers.'

Their revelations of abuse captured in *Who Cares? Young People in Care Speak Out* were widely publicised in 1977 in both the public and professional media. In 1982, NAYPIC in *Sharing Care*, their Evidence to the House of Commons

Committee Inquiry into Children In Care, also wrote about the emotional and physical abuse experience by their members under the official label of 'discipline, punishment and control'. In 1986, NAYPIC submitted Evidence to the Government Review of Residential Care. As well as *Sharing Care*, this included their *Charter of Rights of Young People in Care*. '*The right not to be beaten or have other degrading punishments given*' was the first under 'Rules, punishment and discipline.' In 1990, London NAYPIC published its report, *Abuse in the Care System, a pilot study*, highlighting very high levels of physical and sexual abuse voiced by young people.

But none of these documents, although widely publicised and directed at policy makers, generated the public, professional or political response that would lead to government action to safeguard these young people from 1997. Why was this?

During much of this time, especially the 1970's and 1980's, physical or corporal punishment was seen as acceptable. It wasn't seen as abuse, even though the examples given by young people in this account would today be regarded as serious forms of abuse. This in part reflected societal attitudes towards both 'children and young people' and 'care'. During most of this period, society's attitude towards 'children' as a group was - and perhaps still is - at best ambiguous in terms of respecting, listening, believing, and in effectively and sensitively communicating with them. Societal responses to teenagers were frequently polarised, either reducing them to the passivity of 'children' and 'victims' or elevating them to the culpability of 'adults' and 'villains'. But these were just not any 'children' but children in care. They were children and young people who, in the main, came from very poor families and neighbourhoods, who had experienced neglect, physical or sexual abuse, or difficulties growing up. Not surprisingly a complexity of feelings surrounded their removal to care. They were confused, angry, often frightened and their self esteem was low. As the young people's views in this account reveal, societal attitudes as late as the 1980's, still saw many young people in care as 'blameworthy' and 'criminals' - deserving of punishment.

As we now know, many young people during these years were subject to more serious forms of physical, sexual and emotional abuse that they were unable to speak about. The voices of young people during this story show that many of them felt powerless and stigmatised by their day-to-day experiences of living in children's homes. As Leeds *Ad-Lib, Who Cares?* and NAYPIC uncovered, practices such as institutional clothes stores, 'welfare case' school meals, clothing order books and the bulk buying of everything from sugar to sanitary protection, reinforced a dependency left unchallenged by the increasing confusion as to the role of residential child care within the new order of preventive and diversionary child care services. Not a fertile ground for speaking out.

Also, some young people in care were being subject to 'approved' treatment methods that abused them. The use of regression therapy in some of Leicestershire's children's homes and the so-called Pindown system of control in selected Staffordshire homes became, in effect, sanctioned abuse – although the former represented a crude violation of psychodynamic practice and the latter behavioural therapy. These young people were also let down by the managerial, organisational and inspection systems set up to protect them. These failures included the isolation and lack of accountability of the old approved schools; the failure of social workers to maintain family links; the suppression of complaints by residential staff who 'whistle blow'; the failure of government and local inspections to listen to, or seriously engage with children and young people in care; and the failure to recognise the haunting accounts of older victims, such as Graham Gaskin, and the earlier inquiries, including the Kincora Boys Home in East Belfast.

Care Less Lives?

This story began in 1973. Young people told about their lives in children's homes and residential institutions. For many of these young people 'care' was experienced by them as stigmatising and controlling. They were rarely asked what they thought or involved in decisions about their lives. For the young people who took part in *Who Cares?*, 'care' gave them very little care: not another family who would care for them, not a good education, not skilled help to overcome past difficulties. Instead, their removal to care and the regimes they experienced, led many of these young people to suffer and to blame themselves. It was a care more touched by the poor law than professional vision. But by coming together, sharing their experiences and talking about their lives, young people created *their* rights movement.

By 2003, 30 years later, a lot had changed. Young people in care were far more likely to be living in foster care or very small children's homes. Their rights movement, including its struggles and campaigns over these years, had brought about significant changes in how young people in care were seen: no longer were they to be ignored, they were, as of right, to participate in decisions about their lives. In this respect their care had, over time, been shaped by their own actions and resilience.

But despite these changes, the lives of too many young people still remain *care less* in basic prerequisites: providing young people with a sense of identity and stability in their lives; showing them respect and dignity, by not stigmatising them – from clothing order books in 1973 to bin bags in 2011 - and building a platform for young people to adulthood, as most young people not in care can expect. Young people should also expect to be offered good quality care wherever they live, and not be subject to the territorial injustices that reduce their life chances. Also, as we now know, many of these young people were abused, perverting the rationale of care. A failure to meet young people's needs in these different ways severely undermines their ability to exercise their hard won rights. But, at the same time, it shows why a rights movement for young people in care is needed. The story continues.

Notes and References

Chapter 1 - Why Care Less Lives?

[1] UNCRC (1989) *United Nations Convention on the Rights of the Child*, Geneva, United Nations

[2] From the preface, p9, of E.P. Thompson (1968), *The Making of the English Working Class, Pelican Books*

Chapter 2 - Ad-Lib - Voices from below

[3] See Stein M (Ed) (1977) *Ad-Lib in care group story*, Leeds, University of Leeds. The words of the young people in this chapter are contained within this publication

[4] Pearson, G (1975) *The Deviant Imagination*, London, Macmillan

[5] Stein M (Ed) (1977) p5

Chapter 3 - Who Cares? - 'Spreading the word'

[6] Page, R and Clarke, G (eds) (1977) Who Cares? *Young People in Care Speak Out*, London, National Children's Bureau

[7] Goffman, E (1961) *Asylums*, Harmondsworth, Penguin.

[8] Rowe, J and Lambert, L (1973) *Children Who Wait*, London, ABAFA

[9] DHSS (1974) *Report of the Committee of Inquiry into the Care and Supervision Provided in Relation to Maria Colwell*, London, HMSO

[10] Interview with Rosalind Niblett, NCB Development Worker, Who Cares Project.

[11] The words of the young people presented in this chapter are taken from Page, R and Clarke G (Eds) (1977), cited above.

Chapter 4 - Who cares wins?

[12] National Children's Bureau (1979) *Who Cares? Issues and News*, No 31, London, NCB

[13] Young person's written reflection, dated 27/11.1977

[14] National Children's Bureau (1979) cited above

[15] The articles, poems and views of young people *(There's a Bloke, Who Cares about Public Baths, Leaving Care Poem, Review and Who Cares ?poem)* all appear in National Children's Bureau (1979) cited above

[16] Both the letter and the Daily Mirror response appear in the National Children's Bureau (1979) cited above

Chapter 5 - The National Association of Young People In Care (NAYPIC) - The early years 1979-1983

[17] See National Council for Voluntary Organisations (1984) *Clients' Rights, Report of an NCVO Working Party*, London, NCVO

[18] Parker, L, Stein M, Davies P (1982) 'Ban the Book,' Community Care, 414, 13-14

[19] Children's Legal Centre (1981), Report on the Conference, 'Life in Care,' London, CLC. The views of the young people in this section 'life in Care Conference' appear in this report.

[20] Stein M, and Ellis S, (1983) *Gizza Say, Reviews and Young People in Care*, London, NAYPIC. The views of young people in this section appear in this report.

[21] NAYPIC (1980) *Running an In Care Group, Ideas, Hints, Suggestions for Young People and Social Workers*, Bradford, NAYPIC

Chapter 6 - Sharing care

[22] House of Commons (1984) *Second Report from the Social Services Committee, Session 1983-4, Children In Care*, xiii, London, HMSO

[23] NAYPIC (1983) *Sharing Care*, Bradford, NAYPIC. NAYPIC's evidence is cited in italics, only minor editorial changes have been made.

[24] Letter from Charity Commissioner's to NAYPIC dated 30/12/1982

[25] House of Commons (1984) cited above, cxli

[26] House of Commons (1984) cited above, xiv

Chapter 7 - Black and In care

[27] The Association of Black Social Workers and Allied Professionals, Evidence to House of Commons Select Committee, 1983, Children in Care

[28] Memorandum by the Commission for Racial Equality to House of Commons Select Committee on Children in Care. Cited in House of Commons (1984) cxix

[29] Memorandum by the Association of Black Social Workers and Allied Professionals to the House of Commons Select Committee on Children in Care. Cited in House of Commons (1984) cxix

[30] Commission for Racial Equality (1983) Evidence to the House of Commons Select Committee on Children in Care, p16

[31] Memorandum by the Croydon Race and Community Unit to the House of Commons Select Committee on Children in Care. Cited in House of Commons (1984) cxx

[32] Black and In Care (1985) Black and In Care Conference Report 1984, London, Children's Legal Centre. The views of young people contained within this chapter including the reports from workshops, the poems *Black Rap, Its Bad for your child to be in care*, appear in this report.

[33] Black and In Care (1985) Black and In Care Conference Report 1984, London, Children's Legal Centre.

Chapter 8 - *'Wishes and Feelings'*

[34] For example, Fisher M, Marsh P, and Phillips with Sainsbury E (1986) In and Out of Care, the experiences of Children, Parents and Social Workers, Batsford; Stein and Carey (1986) Leaving Care, Blackwell

[35] House of Commons (1984) *Second Report from the Social Services Committee, Session 1983-4, Children In Care*, xiv, London, HMSO

[36] See, for example, 'Clients Rights, Report of and NCVO Working Party, NCVO, 1984

[37] Denton, A, (1984), *For Whose Eyes Only, files and young people in care*, Bradford, NAYPIC. The views of young people in this section appear in this report

[38] Stein, M and Maynard C, (1985), 'I've never been so lonely' *A survey of young people leaving care*, Bradford, NAYPIC. The views of young people in this section appear in this report

[39] Stein M and Ellis S, (1988), *Guidebooks ND Young People in Care*, Bradford, NAYPIC. The recommendations in this section appear in this report

[40] Sutcliffe T, Berry B, Stein M,(1988) *Care or Control? Sanitary protection and young women in care*, Newcastle, NAYPIC. The views of young people in this section appear in this report.

[41] Wagner (1986) *A Review of Residential Care*

[42] NAYPIC (1986) *Evidence to the Wagner Working Group*, p 4-5, Bradford, NAYPIC

[43] NAYPIC (1986) p5

[44] NAYPIC (1985) *Charter of Rights for Young People in Care*

[45] NAYPIC (1986) p6

[46] NAYPIC (1986) p7

[47] NAYPIC (1986) p7

[48] NAYPIC (1986) p7-8

[49] NAYPIC (1986) p8

Chapter 9 - NAYPIC's Troubles

[50] Letter from DHSS to NAYPIC (15/9/1986)

[51] Letter from DHSS to NAYPIC (26/1/1987)

[52] Letter from DHSS to NAYPIC (5/6/1987)

[53] NAYPIC, Proposals for the Future (26/6/1987)

[54] Funding Application from NAYPIC to the DHSS (30/1/1988)

[55] Letter from DHSS to NAYPIC (21/6/1988)

[56] Letter from DHSS to NAYPIC (6/10/1988)

[57] Letter from the DHSS to NAYPIC confirming the main bullet points (7/11/1988)

[58] Letter from LBGU to In Care Company (2/2/1989)

[59] The letter of 7/11/1988 had stated that *'all future payments (from January 1989) would be suspended unitl such time as NAYPIC's administrative arrangements had been resolved.'*

[60] Letter from the In Care Company to the DHSS (4/4/1989)

[61] Letter from the DHSS to the ICC (20/4/1989)

[62] Letter from the DHSS to the ICC (20/4/1989)

[63] Letter from the DoH to the ICC (7/8/1989)

Chapter 10 - Speak Out '89 - A new beginning?

[64] Hughes, W H, (1985), *Report of the Inquiry into Children's Homes and Hostels.* Belfast, HMSO

[65] Children's Legal Centre (1985) Briefing, *House of Lords Rule on Gillick*, p1, London, CLC

[66] UNCRC (1989) *United Nations Convention on the Rights of the Child*, Geneva, United Nations

[67] This account from the London worker detailed in this chapter is published in Children's Legal Centre, (1989) NAYPIC battle to give young people a voice, *Childright*, 3-4, November.

Chapter 11 - The Aftermath

[68] Community Care (1989) NAYPIC *relaunch ends in conference chaos*, 7/9/1989

[69] Community Care (1989) cited above

[70] Community Care (1989) *Joint forces to heal NAYPIC*, 14/9/1989

[71] Social Work Today (1989) *NAYPIC Independence day flops*, 2/11/1989

[72] Letter from DoH to ICC 9 12/3/1990

[73] Community Care (1990) *A long drawn out battle relentlessly waged*, p6, 19/4/1990

[74] Reported in NAYPIC (1991) NAYPIC, *The Time for Change*, Casework, London, NAYPIC

[75] Funding Application from NAYPIC to the Department of Health (14/121990)

[76] Funding Application from NAYPIC to the Department of Health (14/121990)

[77] Letter from DoH to NAYPIC (12/8/1991)

[78] Letter from DoH to NAYPIC (12/8/1991)

[79] NAYPIC (1991) NAYPIC, *The Time for Change*, London, NAYPIC

Chapter 12 - A National Voice

[80] First Key (1997) *Report to the Department of Health, A National Voice Feasibility Study*, Leeds, First Key

[81] Utting, W, (1997) *People Like Us: The Report of the Safeguards for Children Living Away from Home*, London, Department of Health

[82] First Key (1997)

[83] First Key (1997)

[84] Utting W (1997)

[85] Department of Health (1998) *The Government's Response to the Children's Safeguards Review*, p89, London, Department of Health

[86] Department of Health (1998) *The Quality Protects Programme: Transforming Children's Services*, London, Department of Health

[87] Department of Health (1999) *The Government's Objectives for Children's Social Services*, London, Department of Health

[88] Department of Health (1999) *Me, survive, out there? New arrangements for young people living in and leaving care*, London, Department of Health

[89] A National Voice (1999) *Response to Me, Survive, Out There*, p 22, Manchester, ANV

[90] A National Voice (1999) p22

[91] A National Voice (1999)

[92] A National Voice Business Plan (2001)

[93] A National Voice Business Plan (2001)

[94] Amplify, *All you Need to know about 'Amplify' and a National Voice* (Information Sheet 2002)

[95] A National Voice (2003) *Amplify, 'tell him it's not much fun'* Manchester, ANV

[96] A National Voice (2003) The views of young people in this section are taken from the *Amplify* report

[97] See A National Voice (2003), second edition

[98] Paper from the Department of Health, Functions of' host agency' providing management and support to A National Voice (24/6/2003)

[99] Paper from the Department of Health, Functions of' host agency' providing management and support to A National Voice (24/6/2003)

[100] Butler, P (2003) *Bin the bureaucracy*, Society Guardian, p4 (15/10/2003)

[101] Butler, P (2003) p4

[102] Fleming, J, Gledhill, K, Greaves H, (2003) *Review of a national organisation of young people in care. Report to the DfES*

[103] Letter from the DfES to ANV (26/2/2004)

[104] A National Voice (2005) *There's No Place Like Home*, Manchester, ANV

[105] Please Sir, Can I Have Some More, Education Campaign Survey, ANV, 2005

[106] Please Sir, Can I Have Some More, Education Campaign Survey, ANV, 2005

[107] *These Mater to Us, ANV to Care Matters* consultation, 2007

[108] House of Commons, Children, Schools and Families Committee, Looked After Children, 2008-09, Maxine Wrigley, Chief Executive, A National Voice, witness, 19th March 2008

[109] A National Voice (2010) Emotional Wellbeing Report, ANV

Chapter 13 - From Order Books to Bin Bags

[110] House of Commons (1984)

[111] Page R and Clarke G (1977)

[112] A National Voice (2003)

[113] Page R and Clarke G (1977)

[114] A National Voice (2003)

[115] This section is derived from Stein (2006) Missing Years of abuse in children's homes, *Child and Family Social Work*, 11, pp11-21.